How to Become a
P♠ker Queen

Senior Designer Barbara Zuñiga
Commissioning Editor Nathan Joyce
Production Manager Gordana Simakovic
Picture Manager Christina Borsi
Art Director Leslie Harrington
Editorial Director Julia Charles
Publisher Cindy Richards

Illustrator Rachel Parsons
Indexer Diana Le Core

First published in 2014
by Ryland Peters & Small
20–21 Jockey's Fields
London WC1R 4BW
and
519 Broadway, 5th Floor
New York, NY 10012
www.rylandpeters.com

10 9 8 7 6 5 4 3 2 1

ISBN 978-1-84975-576-4

A CIP record for this book is
available from the British Library.

Library of Congress CIP data has been
applied for.

Printed and bound in China

How to Become a
P◆ker Queen

Rebecca McAdam

RYLAND PETERS & SMALL
LONDON • NEW YORK

Contents

Introduction 6

chapter 1
Setting the Scene 8

chapter 2
Women in Poker 18

chapter 3
Texas Hold 'em 34

chapter 4
Psychology & Strategy 56

chapter 5
Playing Live 74

chapter 6
Playing Online 90

chapter 7
Playing in Tournaments 102

chapter 8
Survival Tips 114

Index 124
Acknowledgments 128

Introduction

My heart was thumping so hard, I could have sworn the guy next to me could hear it.

I weighed up all the possibilities and had decided I had to go ahead with it. His intense stare was intimidating me slightly, but his smirk was egging me on, irritating me. Did he want me to be annoyed? Did he want me to act irrationally? Perhaps he was trying to be cool and play the big guy? What story was he telling me? What stories had he told me in the past? I had thought it through from start to finish, over and over. The odds were fully with me but it seemed like my fingers weren't obeying the instructions from my brain. A few seconds passed, but it felt like an eternity. All eyes were on me, or so it seemed. Just do it, Rebecca, trust yourself, he's bluffing, I told myself. However, at this point, other factors started weighing on my mind, as this one moment could result in polar opposite emotional outcomes: feelings of elation, excitement, confidence, and pride; or regret, sorrow and anguish. Either I was going home to a restless night of what ifs, or I was calling home to say get the champagne out. This was all getting in the way of the feeling that I should do this because I believe it is the right thing to do, even if it turns out bad – the feeling that more often than not, this will be the right thing to do, so I'll just have to take it on the chin if tonight's not one of those nights.

'I'll show you if you fold,' he says, holding his cards up as if he is about to flip them right over, a small bead of sweat passing down one side of his face. 'I call,' I say, not knowing whether it was out loud or to myself. 'Turn over your cards, sir,' says the dealer, making my dreams a reality. And with a look of disgust, my opponent flips over... nada, nothing – it was a complete bluff. The feeling that ensued is one that has never grown old, not even to this day. Years on and that feeling is still the much sought-after cherry at the top of the 'you did good' cake. A common misapprehension is that this feeling is

tied to winning when it comes to poker, but it's really tied to using all your senses and making the right decision, even if that means you have to walk away or lose a little to save you losing it all. It's the pat on the back for trusting your instincts, for adding up all the elements and getting the right answer, for not letting anything sway you from your thoughts and powers of observation, for being right whether that means winning or not.

It is this feeling that truly made me fall in love with poker. The first time.

Setting the Scene

The evolution of poker

Although poker's early history has often been disputed, it's safe to say that its biggest association is with the Wild West. The game is thought to have spread there after becoming a popular feature of the Mississippi riverboats during the Gold Rush period.

When the average Joe or Joanna hears the word poker, it's often hard not to let the mind wander to gun-toting, tobacco chewin', leather-clad cowboys throwing back whiskey in dimly-lit saloons while the women fawn, sigh and heave in the background. Poker, as it is nowadays, has grown quite far from its roots, with technology in the past 10–15 years playing a massive part in the game's metamorphosis. Younger generations may just as easily relate poker with the idea of glossy, late night TV poker reruns, online sign-ups, digital avatars, and the computerized sound of chips making their way across virtual tables – the same *ch-chink* every time. 'GG, WP, UL...' That's text speak for Good Game, Well Played, Unlucky. So how did we get to this point?

Well, really, it was the perfect storm. To set the scene, online poker was starting to garner great attention, while at the same time the game was gaining popularity on TV screens the world over. But what really added fuel to the fire was the success of the aptly-named Chris Moneymaker at the 2003 World Series of Poker (WSOP). The WSOP was born in Las Vegas over 45 years ago and is now the longest running, most prestigious live poker series in the world. The WSOP Main Event is the biggest and most prestigious poker event on this planet, where celebrity poker players sit among unknowns hoping to make their mark. The event is legendary for producing remarkable rags-to-riches stories. This is helped on by the fact that you can qualify into WSOP events via online satellites (poker tournaments that act as cheap gateways into more expensive events) for as little as the change sitting in the cup holder of your car. In this case,

Moneymaker paid $39 into an online satellite on the website PokerStars and won it, earning his ticket into the 2003 WSOP Main Event, his first ever live poker tournament.

What was to follow was truly unbelievable. Just imagine a humble accountant from Atlanta, Georgia, heading off into the sunset to find his Main Event seat worth $10,000 on poker's grandest stage in the midst of the bright lights of Las Vegas. Despite being a complete unknown, his poker skills quickly caught the eye of Lou Diamond, a well-known American sports analyst, who tipped Moneymaker as the dark horse to win the entire tournament. This extraordinary prediction came true, as Moneymaker beat 838 opponents, including many big names in poker. In the final hand of the tournament, he triumphed with a full house and went home with $2.5 million and a WSOP gold championship bracelet. Suffice it to say that he quit his job shortly thereafter...

The press started talking about the 'Moneymaker effect' soon afterwards. Everyone wanted to be a poker hero. Anything was possible. You could be of any age, gender, nationality, race, class; it didn't matter. A good dose of discipline, practice, skill and a splash of luck and you could make your dreams come true. The thinking was 'well, Chris Moneymaker did it – why can't I?' TV Poker exploded pretty much overnight. Card rooms were suddenly filled to the brim. Competition became fierce. Strategy grew rich. Styles varied and trends began. Professional live poker tours spread across the globe. Poker was undergoing a remarkable period of evolution.

Setting the Scene

Turning strangers into friends

As soon as I turned 18, I went straight into a live poker room. I remember it so clearly. I was so nervous and excited. I felt like I did in my first hockey game in school.

We had done all the drills, tested different scenarios, played against each other for weeks, but it was only when we took our new-found skills out into the real world that we really saw how far we had come. I told myself I would only play with a certain amount of money, and I've still never broken that promise. I think this kind of discipline is essential if you want to be a winning player. Unfortunately, it does not only take discipline, or I'd be sipping Piña Coladas at a bar made of coconuts right now... there's a whole lot more. The first place I played live had no frills, no flashing lights, no swanky chairs or tables. I don't get much time these days to get out to it but I hear it's still filled with most of the same faces; a community of people who have been testing their wits against each other for many years.

I remember feeling like an outsider at first, rubbing elbows (literally) with people who were used to a closed clique. Don't get me wrong though, even if I was the odd one out – a young girl in the middle of a room full of men and a couple of older ladies – they, of course, wanted me there because I was fresh blood. If I didn't know what I was doing then it was my own fault and I would have to learn the hard way. Well, nothing worth having comes easy, I say. I swallowed my fear, sat down, and well... I don't remember much. It all happened quite fast. I just remember being there, playing a little, not being very confident, and losing €50 quicker than you can say, 'Stick to the home games, Rebecca.' But it wasn't too busy, so they let me sit and stay at the table to watch for a while. I took in people's styles, their characters, how they reacted to each other, the overall live etiquette and the grand sense of camaraderie; I was hooked and I wasn't even playing!

A couple of weeks later, I was on first-name terms with many of the regulars. The people running the room knew me and they didn't look at me with sympathetic smiles like they once had. I had proven my resilience and willingness to learn. I took note of my mistakes and I adapted. This is another feature of a winning poker player... but yeah, you guessed it, that's still not all you need.

By the time Moneymaker hit the headlines, I was already one of the gang, enjoying my hobby and sharpening my skills. I was now in college, working part-time and spending two nights a week in the poker room. I had other hobbies like going to the movies and I wasn't a big drinker or party-goer. I spent, more often than not, less money on a live poker session than a regular night out, and I had a ton of fun at the tables – meeting people, learning their stories, watching all sorts of dynamics play out. Most importantly there was always something to learn or discover.

The Moneymaker effect had a global impact. Even from the small Dublin club I played in, it was plain to see that the poker world as we knew it was in for a real change. Our small disparate communities were about to be pulled towards each other all around the world. Flocks of new faces appeared in live poker rooms. Hopefuls would tumble in before and after nights out, filled with Dutch courage and inspired by the last TV poker show. Welcome young bucko, take a seat.

Suddenly it was cool to play poker, to be part of the poker world. You put your money where your mouth was and looked your opponent right in the eye (well, sometimes). Wits were tested, sometimes egos, and there was what seemed like an endless amount of money to be won. Times were good. I was, at this point, living well, spending my winnings on holidays and eating out every night. I was lucky to be ahead of the curve and using my edge against those new to the felt. But if I lost what I set out with to spend, then I would shake my fellow poker lovers' hands and go home. I never lost respect for what that first €50 meant to me.

Poker can be broken down into three types of games: flop, draw and stud. Flop games, like Texas Hold 'em and Omaha include community cards. These are cards dealt in the middle of the table, face up, and everyone uses them to make up their hands. Texas Hold 'em is the most popular poker game today. Players are dealt two cards each face-down (known as 'hole' cards) and there are five community cards in total: three are dealt first (this is known as the 'flop' – see the image top right), then one more (called the 'turn'), and then the final card (known as the 'river' – see bottom right). Players must make the best five-card hand using any combination of the seven available to them.

Draw poker hit America in the 1800s and evolved to become the most popular game in the West. Often, it wouldn't just be money that was won and lost. Feuds were triggered and resolved; property, wives and even lives were gambled with! There are no community cards in draw poker; players use only their hole cards. Players can take, or 'draw', new cards from the deck to replace those that they don't want. The variant which kick-started the draw phase in America was Five-Card Draw. Like Hold 'em, with Five-Card Draw, you must make the best five-card hand. You don't get two cards in your hand like in Hold 'em, though, you get five, and you can replace the cards you don't want by drawing new ones during the hand. There are also other variants where you must make the best low hand rather than the best high hand.

The final type is stud. Stud games are those where the player is dealt some cards that are visible to all at the table and some cards that even the player him/herself can't see! This game can get very interesting with the dynamic created from being able to see some of your opponents' cards, and vice versa! It is said that stud had its beginnings in the American Civil War when soldiers played a form called Five-Card Stud. The game has since expanded to a ridiculously long list of variants. Somewhere between draw poker being popular and Hold 'em becoming the game played by the majority, the game of choice was Seven-Card Stud. At the end of a hand of Seven-Card Stud each player ends up with, you guessed it, seven cards – four of these are face up and three are face down. Like Hold 'em, you need to make the best five-card hand, but unlike Hold 'em, you are making the best five card hand out of the seven you're holding, plus aces can be both high and low. Don't forget though, it's not all about what you have; you must take everyone else's cards and actions into account! Sound crazy? It is. Sound fun? Definitely.

Setting the Scene

The 'flop' (below)

Each player has already been dealt 2 private or 'hole' cards, face-down. A round of betting follows, and then 3 community cards (the 'flop') are dealt together, face-up.

The 'showdown' (bottom)

The final community card (the 'river') is dealt face-up. A final round of betting follows and then, assuming that no one has folded, the player with the best 5-card hand (using any combination of the seven available to them), wins.

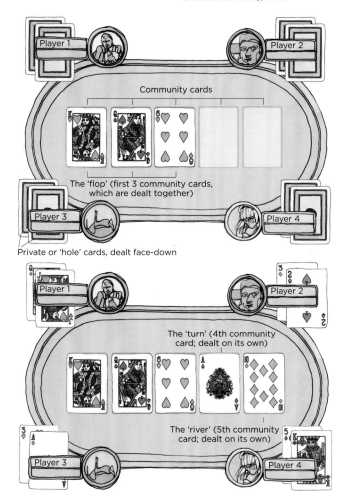

Player 1

Player 2

Community cards

The 'flop' (first 3 community cards, which are dealt together)

Player 3

Player 4

Private or 'hole' cards, dealt face-down

Player 1

Player 2

The 'turn' (4th community card; dealt on its own)

The 'river' (5th community card; dealt on its own)

Player 3

Player 4

Poker today

So alongside the rise of online poker, and poker in general, came a new phenomenon – the celebrity poker pro.

Online sites were popping up everywhere and sponsorships were plentiful; if you had good presence, had an impact on the tables and a few good results, a contract was likely. Young, good-looking, and slightly mouthy? You could be a star! Sometimes the players were not even very good, but if they moved in the right circles, were entertaining and could hold their own, then airtime or at least a free tournament buy-in or two was inevitable. Basically every archetype you could think of, there was, and they were everywhere. They usually had trademarks and adorned themselves in flamboyant outfits, cowboy hats or fancy sunglasses you'd usually see on the slopes. There were those good at magic tricks, the crazy scientists, the femme fatales... you name it, the poker world had it, and we lapped it up. Poker became... well, fabulous, darling.

TV screens in homes the world over introduced us to those who had had a flair for the game long before the cameras came; they had personalities of their own and had risen up the ranks to lead the way into a new horizon. We grew to know poker players by their nicknames, or indeed their alter egos. Home games were filled with chatter about the latest carry-on by the 'Devilfish, 'The Magician', 'Texas Dolly', the 'Unabomber' or the 'Poker Brat'. Professional poker players were becoming celebrities. Poker became entertainment, and it seemed like everyone wanted to be a part of it. Likewise, many 'regular' celebrities outwardly expressed their interest in poker. The game was now being played by people from all walks of life in both everyday and glamorous places, far removed from the outdated image of poker as it once was –

a cowboy's game played by shady characters in dark, smoke-filled basements. Poker was universal, and at the green baize, everyone was equal; that even included the likes of Matt Damon, Ben Affleck, Mena Suvari, Jennifer Tilly and Shannon Elizabeth. Being able to act was not essential, although a good poker face always comes in handy.

   You could call poker more of a hybrid game nowadays; in reference to both how it's played and the types of players playing it. The older generations who learned the game around a live table have since been joined by those who received most of their poker education online. There are those who are experts in reading body language, table talk and manipulation and those who approach the game in a completely mathematical manner, calculating odds rapidly across numerous online tables, or using poker software to help them navigate the battlefield better and faster. A wealth of strategy and information spread after the poker boom, knowledge that many of the older generation would have had to work for years at to gain access to, if at all. If you didn't play online, the chances were you couldn't keep up with the latest trends. Although if you didn't play live, the chances were you wouldn't be prepared for when you did. This led to the online environment clashing with the live. The place we saw conversation and excitement often became quiet and serious. Those who were used to sitting at home playing on their own, switched off the 'noise' at the live felt with headphones, shutting down so as not to give anything away. Old-school poker veterans had to sit next to 21-year-olds with money coming out their ears, and hear about 'five betting' and 'floating' and other terms they perhaps had never heard before. Likewise, the 21-year-olds had to sit next to the veterans who felt their way was 'real' poker and possibly didn't always appreciate the hard work and study being put in, albeit a different kind. This was bound to happen in this technological world we're living in and as the game continues to evolve.

Setting the Scene

Women in Poker

Here come the girls!

For a long time, poker was associated with male bonding and 'manliness' and, unfortunately, that idea has not disappeared. While more and more women are playing at major live poker events, we still have some way to go. It's really just part of women's greater journey to the freedom of being able to fully express who we are and what we wish to do with our time, whatever that may be.

Whatever the rate, the number of women who play poker is increasing. We can see that in live event statistics, and we can also see it with the amount of females raking it in and thrashing it out on the virtual felt. Despite being relatively few in number, we are strong, and have had much success at the baize. Respect levels are growing, but it's up to us to continue this trend and not be deterred. I think back to the time when I first started out – the mixed reaction I got from simply walking to my seat. You could feel the tension that resulted from my presence. There was a spy in the gang; I had broken the sanctity of the boys' night out, the husband's evening away. Should they allow this? Would their wives and girlfriends want to come next? They didn't have to consider this before.

I think back to how things are when I first started and it makes me wonder what women did to carve out their seat at the poker table over 30 or even 40 years ago! In 1978, Barbara Freer became the first woman to enter the World Series of Poker (WSOP) Main Event, which is an open-field event (meaning anyone can play). This was just eight years after Benny Binion set up the WSOP. Four years after this, Vera Richmond was crowned the champion of a WSOP open-field event – the first woman to earn a WSOP bracelet and all the prestige that comes with it. Rumour is she wasn't very popular among her male opponents… I wonder why?! Four years later, in 1986, Wendeen Eolis became the first female to cash in the Main Event – the biggest, most prestigious event in poker, even to this day. These women are inspirational. As are those who followed on from them.

After poker spread and hit screens around the world, more women, and people in general, came to play. Beginners were everywhere 'giving it a go', so it was a great time for the game... and of course for those who knew exactly what they were doing! Aside from watching female celebrities slinging it out with the boys, we also got to witness strong female professionals of the time like Jennifer Harman and Annie Duke in action. Jennifer Harman became the first woman to hold two WSOP bracelets in open events, until 29-year-old Vanessa Selbst equalled this feat while tearing up the felt in 2012. In my early days as a poker enthusiast, I recall buying a chip protector in Las Vegas at the WSOP. It had Annie Duke's signature on it and I was thrilled. The WSOP bracelet holder, author, philanthropist and professional player had inspired me at the time to keep striving forward as one of the few women I knew who played. She would later play across from me in an event, chatting and thrashing it out as she always has. I still have the chip protector.

Part of the initial inclusion of women in poker tournaments was to add glamour and intrigue and to broaden the appeal to audiences. Sadly, female players were also judged on appearance, and their actions were often scrutinized more than their male opponents, but that is something that continues today inside and outside of poker. As the Canadian politician Charlotte Whitton once said, 'Whatever women do they must do twice as well as men to be thought half as good. Luckily, this is not difficult.'

Women in Poker

A gender-less game

The invention of online poker helped to break the gender barrier down further. The computer screen removed the involvement of gender, physical appearance, and social behaviour from the game. Players had female or male avatars but that didn't really tell you anything as, it's sad but true, many men had female avatars in the hopes of taking advantage of assumptions that would be made about the way they played. However, women could often be guilty of this psychological game-play, which was based purely on stereotypes of both sexes too. There really should never be any reason to de-feminize ourselves or to try to act more like men. There is a happy balance we can find by playing our own game using our own natural skills and insights, and that really goes for anything in life.

Following the boom, poker continued to grow, and with that the standard rose. Over the years, amazing female talent came to the fore – incredible women on our screens and in the news being successful, doing extraordinary things, and having their voices heard.

Over the past 10 years or so poker tours have expanded across the globe; that includes championships traversing the world, and big festivals focusing on a certain area, pulling into various cities once per season. In my time with Poker Magazine and website Card Player, I worked as a one-woman army covering each stop of the European Poker Tour (EPT); getting the interesting stories for the European magazine and reporting the latest updates live. When it came to female success, I found I was often pulled between wanting to encourage and inspire by highlighting the role models we had out there, and not wanting to overly celebrate for fear of further separating the genders. Journalist, presenter and poker player Vicky Coren was the first woman to win an EPT Main Event. In 2014, Vicky

went on to win another EPT Main Event – a feat no other player in the world has achieved. In-between Vicky's first victory and most recent, there were two more female EPT champions: Sandra Naujoks from Germany, and Liv Boeree from England, and I got to witness them both. I couldn't help but ask, 'How do you feel to be the second woman/the third woman to win an EPT?' Whereas some female players are happy to talk about their success in relation to both their gender and the game as a whole, others see even the mention of this as a backwards step. I can see it from both points of view. I don't believe in celebrating the last woman standing in an open event for instance, although if her story is interesting and she's a good player, I want to know about her. I do, however, think that women have a certain responsibility to each other and if they have etched their names in history as the first or the fifth or the 12th then that's great.

One day a female winner will be just another winner, but to get there we need more women, like you. Then together we can strive towards changing the status quo.

Poker playing styles

Although everyone plays differently, it's useful to take a look at how players in general can be categorized. Terms such as 'tight', 'loose', 'passive', and 'aggressive' are often used to describe identifiable styles of play.

Tight means the person plays conservatively and does not part with their chips easily. They usually fold a lot and don't get involved in very many hands. A loose player is quite the opposite. This person will get involved in the action quite a bit.

An aggressive player will usually be the dominant player in many hands, leading the way and making his/her presence felt. A passive player, well... is just that. He/she will call and check most of the time rather than bet high and raise. But only a fool would lock people into categories, as many players know their own style and how they are perceived; therefore, they can change their style mid-game and take advantage. This is a great skill to have in your locker.

These four traits can be combined to form playing styles. It is not necessarily a good thing to be both loose and passive. This means you tend to get involved in a lot of hands (including some you shouldn't), and as you play more like a follower rather than a leader, you don't make good use of the times you actually have the best hand. Tight and passive means you don't get involved very much and when you do it's only really with the top range of hands; when you're in on the action, you do not act aggressively enough, meaning that you'll miss out on picking up chips. Many beginners are either loose and passive or tight and passive. This is probably due to the lack of knowledge about what hands they should be playing in the beginning. However we all have to learn somehow and as we do we can always change! Tight, aggressive (TAG) players don't play a lot of hands but when they do you'll know about it. They have a smaller range of hands that they play and they strike while the iron is hot. When they have 'it', they ensure they get maximum value for it. Although sometimes what they are doing can become transparent if they don't mix it up.

Loose aggressive (LAG) players are generally fearless, but this can be both a good and a bad thing. They are active a lot of the time and can bluff a fair bit, but are, in turn, difficult to bluff. They can be quite hard to read as they play a wide range of hands. However they can walk themselves into trouble with this style; if a LAG player continually doesn't believe you, all you need is the right hand to do some damage.

Although poker styles can be lumped into categories, there really is no one correct way to play, so feel free to try out different styles until you find one that works for you.

Preconceptions

There are many preconceptions about female poker players. While this sounds like a really bad thing, if your opponents want to use the information they believe to be true about you against you rather than the information you are actually presenting, then this can actually be of great use to you. There are many instances like this where you can use stereotypes and perceived weaknesses to your advantage. Simply put, let them think what they like while you take their chips fair and square. Why not use your opponent's ignorance against them?

Women in Poker

The common misapprehension is that a woman's playing style is fairly inflexible, and that we'll only be aggressive when we see 'pretty' (i.e. picture cards). Women have often been labelled as having a tight style of play or being 'nitty', meaning that they don't part with chips too easily. There is also the idea that we can be easily scared off. This means we can be tested frequently. Our opponents can try to run over us even if they have nothing or next to it because if we are not entirely strong (in the cards sense) we'll fold rather than calling, and will certainly never re-raise. Oh and the other stereotype is that we don't or can't bluff. If we're betting, we have to have it. We certainly wouldn't take a risk like that with nothing... would we?! Sigh...

Ok, I'll back off... a little. Not everyone thinks this way. Most experienced male players treat their female opponents the same as anyone else. In my experience, the more professional the player, the less likely he/she is to make the mistake of making assumptions, especially those based on gender. The thing is, yes, perhaps a lot of women could be tight, passive players, but that's probably because a lot of them are beginners or in the first stages of honing their game and finding their own style. There are just as many men, if not more, who play like this. It's just easier to notice women's play as we are the obvious minority in a very male-dominated environment. Maybe it's that some men, because of culture and history, have come to expect women to submit to them in poker as they have in the past in other areas of life, especially as poker is such a traditionally male realm. Let's just take a basic look at what poker is about, though. It's not a game of brawn or who has the biggest balls. So take away the Wild West saloon environment it has previously been associated with and what do you have? A game for anyone and everyone. A game of skill, calculation, psychology, observation and focus. A game that once we learn we can play whatever damn style we like. And if some of our male opponents still like to think of us as weak, well then so be it, we'll just have to let the chips do the talking.

Success stories

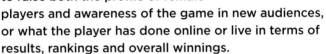

There are so many players who come to mind when I think about female success in poker over the years. Of course, you could either measure success by what someone has done to raise both the profile of female players and awareness of the game in new audiences, or what the player has done online or live in terms of results, rankings and overall winnings.

Despite the pool of female players being quite small in the overall scheme of things, we actually have oodles of amazing talent from all around the world representing us out there every day – more than this book has space for. In saying that, it's hard for Vanessa Selbst's name not to spring to mind. The New Yorker with a law degree from Yale, has been playing poker for over 10 years and is not only the highest earning female poker player of all time, but one of the highest earning poker players of all time. As well as being a very likeable character and a formidable force on the live and online poker scene, Vanessa's statistics are truly out of this world. Still under 30 years of age, Vanessa had earned over $10 million. In 2010, Vanessa, who is sponsored by online poker site PokerStars, earned two first places and a fourth in live events which earned her almost $3 million. Among her successes, you will also find three WSOP bracelets, the most recent of which she won in May 2014, along with the small matter of $871,148. The list is quite small of those who have won multiple bracelets in open events at the WSOP; and even smaller is the number of women on that list (2).

The list of top female earners of course includes Kathy Liebert and Jennifer Harman, names that have been around poker for many years. These American professionals have over $5 million and $2.6 million in earnings respectively and a list of groundbreaking achievements. A name that entered the poker world in a different way to the likes of Kathy is Annette Obrestad. Annette rose to the fore via online poker. The Norwegian, who was born in 1988, started playing when she was 15 years old and claims to have built her online bankroll from nothing. Annette made headlines when she won an online tournament after claiming only to have looked at her cards once. She then garnered even more respect when she became the youngest player to gain a WSOP bracelet. She did this by winning the Main Event of the very first WSOP Europe, the day before her 19th birthday, in 2007.

Also in the upper echelons of the top female earners is Vanessa Rousso. Vanessa, another member of Team PokerStars Pro, was born in New York and graduated from Duke University in just two and a half years. She studied law for a time before hitting the poker felt and raking in more than $3.4 million in winnings. She has been involved in the poker education of women by holding boot camps and training sessions.

Rock chick Liv Boeree studied astrophysics and science before becoming the third female to win a European Poker Tour (EPT) Main Event when she topped a field of 1,239 players in San Remo in 2009. The $1.25 million she received was her biggest score to date, but that was certainly not her only payday, with over $2.4 million in tournament winnings.

If we're talking about achievements, then look no further than Vicky Coren. Vicky has been a staple of the poker world for many years. She hit the limelight in 2006 when she took down the EPT London Main Event for a payday of £500,000. Eight years later and the Team PokerStars pro showed no sign of slowing down, raising up the EPT trophy once again and pocketing €476,100 this time in San Remo. The well-known columnist, panellist, presenter and poker player has had many nice cashes and results in the interim, but the big deal here is that up until her, no player has ever won two EPT Main Events. They tried; they came close, but ultimately couldn't go all the way the second time around. Vicky could. And she did with style: a true model for women inside and outside of poker.

Overcoming prejudice

I was part of a generation who left school thinking that I could be who I wanted and I could do whatever I wanted. With that in mind, it was an eye-opener for me to see that sexism still existed.

When I first started playing, I found myself asking permission to join games, because all the regulars were men, and it felt like women were not allowed. I have sat at poker tables in respectable clubs and been repeatedly asked, 'You must be here because your boyfriend plays, right?'. Another time, I wreaked havoc on the felt in a pub tournament and heard two of my opponents say 'We shouldn't allow women to play in this anymore.' I have been given every reason under the sun as to why a guy lost to me instead of him admitting, even just to himself, that he was outplayed. It's ok if a girl beats you. Really.

On two occasions men have tried to give me chips.... like lollipops at the doctor's. No thanks; I'll probably make them mine soon anyway with that attitude! Male players often try to push me around thinking a big bet is going to scare me off. This can usually be very rewarding. I have been scrutinized, pestered, and one time verbally abused at the poker table. But that is really a rarity nowadays. If anything like that does happen, the dealer or tournament staff will jump in. That occasion turned out to be a great lesson in keeping my cool. In the end it was Mr. Big Mouth and I, head to head for the top prize, and let's just say it didn't end too well for him. I was glad I had not stooped to his level, and the pride I felt at how I managed myself and my game was indescribable. His fear and insecurities had distracted him from the task in hand. I guess that was his lesson to learn.

If you google 'women and poker', references to sexy female players are slowly being drowned out by positive, intelligent articles. I guess the 'she's a girl, so let's talk about how she looks' take on things is something that's not going to vanish overnight, though. It's pretty sad considering those who are doing the judging. Trust me, poker is not brimming with the athletic, dashing kind. And what does it matter anyway? I'm actually fine with the sexy references, if these articles are highlighting ladies who are in the game because they're passionate, talented contributors to the industry. I'm not fine with it, however, if it's a model who was approached to be the face of a poker site and thinks Texas Hold 'em is a raunchy, barn dance. You would never see a professional male poker player on the cover of a magazine holding cards shyly up to his face with a coy half smile and his abs on show. Thankfully, the poker media these days are focusing on more significant issues when it comes to female players, like the quality of play, achievements and longevity – a sign of changing times.

Professional poker player Katie Stone founded female poker team, The Grindettes, after becoming fed up with seeing the wrong women getting coverage. She felt that this was cementing the view that women in poker were to be regarded for their looks and not their ability or accomplishments. Katie wanted to show the world that women of all types could play poker and be profitable. By forming the team, Katie wanted to tell the world: 'Look, we are here. We exist. We are not idiots, and we are not going to wear a bikini for photographs on top of a poker table. We are going to play poker with you and compete head to head just like everyone else.'

The poker world had come a long way; even since one of my earliest magazine cover stories when I asked the player the first question and almost as soon as he started, he stopped and asked, 'Do you know poker or...?' My eyes glazed over. The assumption was we didn't. Having said that, I've found that on the table, men's assumptions are often costly and they have paid the price for it with their chips.

Kara Scott is a presenter, journalist and poker enthusiast. On top of having all the characteristics of a successful poker player, Kara is humble, kind, clever, and has presence.

Most presenters in poker are attractive women and it used to be that the commentary and analysis was left to the boys. This has changed drastically and now you will find women who play, present, and write. Kara Scott does all of the above. She talks the talk while gracefully walking the walk. Among her many achievements, she won the PartyPoker.com Sports Stars Challenge III, and finished second in the 2009 PaddyPowerPoker.com Irish Open Main Event for more than $400,000. In 2009 she joined Team Party and can be seen on the live felt, in the online news, and on television regularly.

Here is where Kara's story began: 'I had just finished filming a TV series about Backgammon when a small cable channel in the UK saw my work and asked me to come in and audition for a TV show called Poker Night Live. The job sounded fun, but I quickly realised that it wasn't something that I could fake. I took a deep breath and at the risk of losing the job, I told them I knew nothing at all about the game. Luckily, that's exactly what they were looking for!

My job was to host a live TV show that revolved around poker pros watching footage from online tournaments and commentating their way through them. My role was to act as the novice (easy!) and to ask the questions that new viewers and players would want to ask. I spent hours upon hours watching poker hands play out and listening to a variety of pros talk strategy. It was like being paid to get high level coaching! Eventually, all of that instruction began to sink in and I started to play a little bit myself. I read as many poker books as I could get my hands on, I read poker forums and I started watching strategy videos for beginners. I was hooked.

When I first picked up a deck of cards, the whole game seemed to be a kind of foggy mystery to me. I was convinced that I'd never be able to learn the 'secret' of good players. Finally, it dawned on me. There really is no secret formula. The answer turned out to be, like pretty much anything in life, study and effort. And honestly, I think it's more fun that way. There is something intoxicating about being able to see your own progression and earning a level of mastery through sweat and hard work. Poker is like the best puzzle you'll ever attempt to solve because the solution is constantly changing.

Women in Poker

After my Poker Night Live days, I moved into other TV in England and Europe and was lucky enough to become an ambassador for partypoker as well as taking on the host duties for their shows like The Big Game and the Premier League. Never one to sit back and get comfortable, I managed to push my way into a meeting with a producer in the USA and convince him to give me a shot. I've been very lucky indeed to work with the talented people at Poker PROductions who film the World Series of Poker for ESPN. The first time I stood in front of the ESPN cameras with an audience of over a million people watching, I couldn't help looking back to 2006 and my first stumbling shows on Poker Night Live and be truly grateful for the industry that had become my home.

Poker has given me a lot. Not only have I been able to pursue my TV career in directions that I never would have thought possible, but I've also had some great success at the poker tables, met an enormous amount of interesting, talented and creative people and have travelled the world.'

chapter 3
Texas Hold 'Em

Poker ingredients

There are a few crucial components that make up any game of poker – players, cards, betting (see page 46 for more about this) and rules. Let's start by breaking down the rules of Texas Hold 'em – what is it really all about?

In Texas Hold 'em, each player is dealt two cards, called 'hole' cards. The game is played in a clockwise motion. The dealer deals the cards to the players this way, one at a time, and the players take turns acting in this direction also. This means once the player on your right makes their move, it's your turn. You don't have to play these two cards but you must wait until it's your turn before you do anything.

A small, white round disc often with the word 'button' or 'dealer' on it is rotated clockwise and indicates where the dealer is at the table. The dealer is the last player to act in each hand. In live tournaments, however, there is usually a dedicated dealer – therefore the button represents the player who would normally be the dealer in a home game. When a full hand is played out, the button moves one space to the left and that player becomes the dealer (last to act). The button was also once known as the 'buck'. The expression 'passing the buck', meaning the transference of responsibility for your own actions to another person, is thought to have originated from poker.

Once everyone has their two cards, betting can begin (explained in more detail on page 46). At any time, you can abandon your interest, known as 'folding' in the current hand, by either communicating verbally that you 'fold' to the dealer or by moving your hole cards in to the muck (see right). When the first round of betting is finished, the chips are moved into the centre of the table. This is known as the 'pot'. This, and what could yet be added in subsequent rounds of betting, is what you're playing for. Well... often along with pride, ego, redemption, revenge and bragging rights, to name but a few things at stake at the poker table! But to be a good poker player you must stay focused on the task in hand and leave your baggage at the door.

So, a pot now sits in the middle of the table and we are about to see the first lot of community cards. The dealer discards the top card from the deck (known as 'burning') and moves it to one side, face down; the discarded cards are kept together in what is usually referred to as the 'muck' (this process helps to protect against forms of cheating, such as card marking). Then, the dealer deals three cards face up in the centre of the table. This is called the 'flop'.

There is another round of betting before the dealer 'burns and turns' again. This fourth community card is called the 'turn', also known as 'fourth street'.

More betting occurs here before the dealer burns the top card of the deck again for the last time and deals the final community card face up on the table. This final community card is called the 'river', also known as 'fifth street'. The final round of betting then takes place and a winner emerges. Out of those still involved in the hand (i.e. everyone who has not folded), the person with the best five-card hand out of all seven (five community cards and two hole cards) is the victor of that hand. They get to take the pot and then the next hand is dealt. This is a description of a full hand if it plays out until the end. Depending on the situation, play can end or indeed peak anywhere along the way – the betting could end before anyone even sees the flop (if everyone but the aggressor lays down their hand) or you could find yourself with nothing else to bet before you see all the cards – for instance if you didn't have very many chips left. That's where the term 'all in' might come in handy! (see page 45 for more about this)

Introducing Hold 'Em

Poker as a category is pretty extensive; it involves numerous games, all with cards, rankings, betting and strategy. But when Moneymaker's story caught the attention of the mainstream audience and movies like Rounders reminded the world of how exciting poker could be, it became all about Texas Hold 'em.

The game's origins are in its name but it wasn't too long before it had spread to Las Vegas where it drew the attention of the likes of American poker greats Doyle Brunson and Amarillo Slim. The legendary Mr. Brunson, also known as 'Texas Dolly', has seen all the changes Texas Hold 'em has gone through – from the days where sometimes it was the armed robber and not the winner who took home the goods, to the glamour of live events and sponsored professionals, the boom of televised poker shows with hole-card cameras showing viewers at home what players were holding, to the 21-year-olds who don't even have to leave their homes to make a living.

Hold 'em is the most popular poker game nowadays by a long shot. It is by no means the only poker game around – there are plenty of options to choose from, but I guess you could call it the English language of the poker world. You could get card players of all different types from all over the world together in the same room, and the poker game the majority would be able to play together is Texas Hold 'em. The different types of games are a good way of further educating and entertaining yourself, but there is a lifetime and more of learning in this one game on its own. Hold 'em never ceases to amaze me – from its strategy, to the events surrounding it, to the people hoping to 'solve' it, and the stories those who play it have to tell. It's a great place for a new player to start as focusing on Hold 'em will give you a mutual language to speak with all the other poker lovers of this world, but I will also give you a taste of what else there is out there to prepare you if you choose to go exploring other variants.

How the table is set up

Texas Hold 'em can be played as a cash game or in a tournament style. It is a multiplayer game where you could have up to ten players at a table, or you could just be playing it with one other (known as 'heads up').

There could be dozens of tables of players doing this all at once or just the table you're on. You may get to know one table after some time of play in the same seat, but that then may change as players get knocked out or get moved. Then you must adapt and start learning about someone new or adjust to a new table dynamic. Whatever the format, the game can completely change at any given moment, so there

really is never a situation you cannot learn from. It is a game that needs thought, concentration and patience but it's also surprising, adrenaline-inducing and fun. You can be yourself, you can be someone else, you can decide to be more ballsy or even less ballsy than you would be normally or accentuate other qualities you think might make an impact on your success rate. It can make you start thinking about life on a whole new level, helping you to better analyse or navigate situations outside of poker. Learning how to play and improving your game all just takes a little time and practice, and during that time it will test you, stress you, and often frustrate you. One thing it won't do is bore you.

So, how is it decided which player acts first and how does the betting begin? Well, both these questions are answered by two things: the 'button' and the 'blinds'. In home games or self-dealt games, the person with the button (see page 36) usually deals the hand. However, in tournaments where there is a professional dealer, or online where the cards are automatically dealt to each player, the button just marks where the dealer would normally be. The person in this position is the last person to act in a hand and so gets to see what everyone else does first. As poker is largely about getting as much information as possible to make the most-informed decisions, this is the best position you can be in. Beside the button are the small blind and the big blind. Blinds are compulsory bets to get the action going, and they come around to each player in turn. The small blind is normally half the big blind. The dealer deals the cards clockwise starting with the small blind.

The best thing for you to do is to go and play with your friends. If you can't get out to play or you're feeling a little overwhelmed, have a look at some poker shows or perhaps play a little online – it won't be long before you get a feel for the game and are raring to get in on the action.

Texas Hold 'Em

Positions at the table

Position in poker is extremely important, and some positions are better than others. Every player at a poker table takes turns holding the various positions as the button moves around in a clockwise motion. The later you are to act in a hand the better, as you're getting as much information as possible before making a decision.

The poker table can be segmented into three groupings of positions – early, middle and late. The worst position to be in is the earliest, the one to the left of the blinds. This player is the first to act at the table. This position is called 'under the gun' (or UTG for short). This player has no information to work with, only the cards in his or her hands, so generally should not get involved in betting with a weak hand (see pages 48–53 for more information about this). A great hand in this position is of course better and worth playing but you will still be 'out of position' instead of being able to react, so you'll be acting without really knowing where you stand. It is best to play fewer hands in early position and better to stick to the top range of hands when or if you do.

The next person to act is generally referred to as 'under the gun +1' (or UTG+1) – not really a great position, either, as they don't have much more information than UTG. The good news, however, is that things look better the further we go around the table and the closer we get to the button, which is the best position you can have. Players in late position, like the button, can try to steal the blinds if they so desire. If there is no action and it comes back around to the dealer, he/she may raise with the idea that those after him/her will fold, giving up their blinds to the aggressor. The term 'defending your blind' comes into play here. Some players may not fold and will call to see the flop – defending their blind.

The next best spot at the table to the button is the one just before it. This is known as the 'cutoff'. In this position you can get a lot of information before acting and you can also spoil

any plans the button may have of raising by making your own move, essentially 'stealing' their position. A play like this is not as obvious when done from the cutoff as it is when done from the button. The player to the right of the cutoff is known as the 'hijack'. In this position you can take away the cutoff's potential steal by trying out one of your own.

'Having position' on a player means you are on their left and you get to act after them. This means you are 'in position' in the hand, somewhere you always want to be, especially if your opponent is an aggressive player. This way you will get to see what they do before you act. In any given hand, where you are in the betting sequence will make all the difference.

Speaking about position, professional poker player Melanie Weisner says: 'Being "in position" lets you bet your hands with more accuracy, and have more control over the final pot sizes and showdowns. When you play a hand in position, it is your decision to call a bet, raise a bet, or give a free card. Because you have the knowledge of their action and they don't have the knowledge of yours, your decisions become much easier. You can play a wider range of hands in position than out of position, as you will need to combat the disadvantage of being out of position with stronger hand strength.'

Betting

When playing poker, there are a number of different actions you can make when it's your turn to do so.

To 'check' means you're staying involved in the hand but not taking further action. You are essentially electing to see more cards without betting anything, but with the option to act at a later stage. You can only check if you are not faced with a bet.

To 'call' simply means that you will match the previous bet. To 'raise', well, that's pretty obvious. However, you should know that there is usually a minimum raise: the standard rule to raising is you must raise by at least the amount of the previous raise. Players can re-raise, also known as three-betting... and this can keep going with four-betting and five betting. However it can only last so long, as you don't have a never-ending well of chips! But let's not get too ahead of ourselves here. I want to prepare you to hold your own on the felt, not to become an aggressive maniac who likes to put their chips in the middle every few minutes. As we've already mentioned, to 'fold' means you're bowing out of this round and will wait until the next hand is dealt. However, it doesn't mean that you can start playing Angry Birds on your phone or to look around the room to see if there is anyone you know. You should be observing your opponents – what they do in this hand could be of value to you in the next!

Betting always begins with the player to the left of the big blind. The player to the left of the big blind can decide to call the big blind, raise or fold. Players can now call, raise or fold in turn until it gets back to the small blind.

Once the blinds pass you, and the player to your left is now the small blind and you are the button, there will be a few hands where you will be able to see your cards without having to give away any of your chips. When the blinds come around however, you have to pay without having seen your cards yet.

The small blind has the option of matching the most recent bet by calling, or if there were no bets they can just complete the blind i.e. match the big blind. However if the big blind then decides to raise it up, the small blind has another decision to make. Other options are raising or folding – of course you don't have to play just because you have some chips out there. The player in the big blind already has the minimum bet out so can decide to call or raise any previous bets, or if the action has been relatively tame and there has been no betting, he/she has the option of checking. There is no point in folding here if you are the big blind and are not faced with a bet – you're getting to see more cards at no extra cost. As my mother says, never look a gift horse in the mouth! However, if the action has been quiet you may decide to throw a spanner into the works and raise it up!

'Antes' are another type of bet that can come into play. They are compulsory bets that are enforced in a tournament after a while, and every player must pay them, whether in addition to blinds or not. They are put out for the dealer to collect before he/she deals the cards to the table.

Finally, let's get down to it. The be-all and end-all bet. The 'I'm putting everything on the line' bet. The 'all-in'. This is when a player puts everything they have left over the line and will either end up busting out or gaining a heck of a lot more chips, if players call and lose. It's a heart thumper! What's more sweat inducing than moving all-in? Calling an all-in! You want to be the one making this move first. Being the one to call can be extremely stressful, unless you're holding the nuts (the best hand) then you should snap-call (call instantly). There are very few intense moments like being all-in for your tournament life and waiting to see if you win or lose. Sometimes in life you just have to go with what you believe in and put a big decision on your opponent.

Hold 'em variants

So you're starting to get an idea of this Texas Hold 'em business, now what? Well, there are a few different types of Hold 'em formats but the basics (two hole cards, five community cards) don't change. The difference is all in the betting structure.

Let's start with the most popular version – No-Limit Texas Hold 'em or 'NLH' as the dudes who like to 'abbrev' say. No limit means just that; there is absolutely no limit to the betting at any point. Anyone can go all-in at any time. This means you could dramatically increase your stack or go bust in any hand. The minimum raise is to raise by at least the amount of the previous raise. The maximum bet is everything you have in front of you. You can of course bet anywhere in between there also. This means No-Limit is often the most dramatic kind to play and watch with its explosive pots, massive bluffs, and overall, more aggressive action.

Before NLH became so popular, the poker crowd swayed more towards Pot or Fixed Limit Hold 'em. Fixed limit Hold 'em sees a strict betting structure with a cap on the amount you can bet and the number of times you can do it. The norm is you can bet up to four or five times in a betting round, but this depends on the rules where you play. There is a small bet and a big bet in Fixed Limit Hold 'em. Whatever the blinds are will determine this, and the blinds are usually bigger than in NLH. The big blind equals the small bet - this is used preflop and on the flop. If a player wants to raise here then they simply add another small bet on top. The big bet is double the small bet i.e. double the big blind. This comes in on the turn and river where betting changes to increments of the big bet. Although this fixed betting structure can mean you can't get into too much trouble, it also means you can't apply too much force whenever you wish. Therefore it's a game of real patience and maths, where you build your stack slowly, by playing the good hands strongly and letting the weaker hands go.

In Pot-Limit Hold 'em, you can build the pot throughout the hand, which could result in you eventually going all-in if you wish. The minimum bet is the same as the big blind, and the minimum raise means to raise by at least the amount of the previous raise. The maximum bet is the same amount as the pot – and the 'pot' is considered to be what's in the middle of the table, on top of what has been bet previously in that round, plus the amount it would take to call the last bet. There is no cap on the amount of times you can raise, unlike in Fixed Limit.

Pot-limit plays out like a crescendo. It starts off subtle, restricted in its movement, but then usually builds to a peak, allowing drama to ensue. What a player can do early on in a hand is limited by the amount he or she can bet, but as the hand develops, tasty pots can be built. It can start out cheap which means more players may come along, but it can get expensive very quickly. One annoying thing about it, though, is that if you do not have a big stack and need to be aggressive, there is only a certain amount of force you can apply early on.

The hands

Anything can happen in poker and that's what makes it so exciting. With 52 cards in a deck, and a variety of games, formats and rules, the combinations and situations are endless – and that's without adding a bunch of personalities to the mix. There are always lessons to be learned; even the most experienced professional has to keep on top of the game through constant study and self-analysis. But that's getting a bit ahead of ourselves. I think a good place to start is by looking at the types of hands one can make, or indeed pretend to make, in poker.

There is a standard hand ranking system in poker which goes from best to worst, top to bottom. You rarely see the best, and it's a sight for sore eyes when you do – just make sure your opponents can't tell how fast your heart is beating if you get there. The 'worst' in this case may be the least attractive when looking at the overall ranking but is not to be ruled out. It can often be good enough, depending on the situation. So it's worth noting that although this graph may look like the bottom hands are weak, you are not always playing against the higher-ranked hands. Often it's not about the cards at all, but the person behind them or the actions they make. Can you make them believe you have better by the story you are telling despite what you are holding? Did they hit what they wanted to or are they just pretending? There is potential power in your hand no matter what it is because poker is so much more than just cards.

In poker, hands are constructed from a total of five cards; no suit is better than the next, and an ace can be both low and high. Let's talk through the hands from top to bottom.

Royal Flush – the cream of the crop. The shooting star of the green-felted sky. The Loch Ness Monster of the poker swamp. This miraculous hand comprises five cards in a row from 10 through to ace that all belong to the same suit. It comprises both a straight and a flush – the highest-ranking straight flush you can get.

Straight Flush – five consecutive cards is a 'straight'. Five cards belonging to the same suit is a 'flush'. Put them together and blow me over, you have a 'straight flush'. In the event of two straight flushes on the table, the one with the highest 'top' card wins.

Four-of-a-kind – this is also known as 'quads'.

It is four cards of the same ranking. It usually doesn't matter what the fifth card is – this card completes and often supports your hand and is known as a 'kicker'. However on this occasion the four cards really speak for themselves. You would be truly unlucky to be up against someone with a higher four-of-a-kind or a better hand overall.

Full House – this is sometimes called a 'boat' –

three cards of the same rank with two cards of another; so basically three-of-a-kind plus a pair. This example is the best full house possible; aces full of kings, but once you make a hand as strong as a full house, you'll be smiling and applying for that mortgage.

Flush

– five cards all of the same suit, but not in any particular order. The highest card determines the rank of the flush; therefore an ace-high flush is the best kind of flush a girl could have.

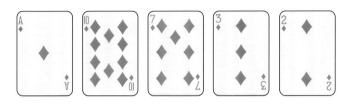

Straight

– five consecutive cards. Here's a good example of where an ace can act as either a high card or a low card. For instance you can have a straight that runs A, 2, 3, 4, 5 but you can also have one that runs 10, J, Q, K, A. You always want to have better than your neighbour if you believe or calculate that they are on to the same thing, therefore the higher the better. However a straight is a straight and is not to be scoffed at.

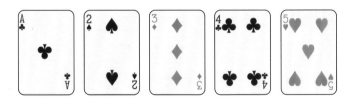

Three of a kind

– Three matching cards. Here we have three sevens. The best three of a kind is three aces and the worst is three twos, poor little duckies. However those ducks will do you good when all someone has is a pair or two. If two of the cards are in your hand and you are using just one from the board then you should really say you have made a set. If one card is in your hand and two are on the board, you have hit trips. This is getting technical, though, so for now just know that three of a kind is often a powerful hand despite being the fourth lowest on the scale.

Two Pair

– Does what it says on the tin. Two cards of the same rank plus two cards of the same rank. The highest pair is what leads the way and determines the rank of your overall hand.

One Pair – Two cards of the same rank with aces being the best pair around.

Ace-high – Sometimes all a player needs is a good high card, and a simple ace up your sleeve is not always that bad – not literally though, as we can't have you being kicked out on my behalf for your magic skills. You'd rather have something more but there are occasions where an ace is all you need.

Poker jargon

Categorizing Players/People

Calling Station - A player who likes to call... a lot; these players don't normally raise, they simply check and call

Fish/Donkey – Not a very good player

Maniac – A loose player. Likes to gamble a lot. Aggressive.

Nit/Rock – A tight, conservative player. Tough to get chips from.

Railbird – An observer on the outskirts of the action

Shark – Be warned, this player knows what they're doing

Whale – A weak player with a lot of money

Good Things

Card Rack – Player on a hot streak of nice cards

Hero Call – To make a big call with a weak hand going on gut/your read and believing your opponent is bluffing or extremely weak

Nuts – The best hand

A Walk – Everyone folds to the big blind, giving him/her 'a walk' (a baseball play when a batter is entitled to walk to first base after being thrown four pitches outside the strike zone)

Waking Up With a Hand – You have been dealt two nice hole cards

Bad Things

Angle Shooter – Acts underhandedly in order to get ahead

Bad Beat – When your opponent gets lucky to come from behind and beat you

Chip Dumping – Losing chips to another player on purpose. Against the rules.

Drawing dead – You are behind, and you're going to stay that way

Leaks – A flaw or weakness in your game

Misclick – Making a mistake during online play by clicking the wrong button. Can be heard or used on the live felt also.

Slow Play – A player acting weak despite having a good hand. Basically the opposite of bluffing. Only bad when it's done to you.

Tilt – Usually occurs when things aren't going well for a player. A physical and mental state that negatively impacts decision-making.

Texas Hold 'Em

Actions

Call The Clock – The 'clock' is there to protect players from taking too long with their decision. Calling the clock on someone will result in a tournament director coming to the table and counting down a set time that the player must make their decision in.

Coin Flip/Race – Two players, who are both all-in and have an equal (or close to equal) chance of winning the pot

Floating – Calling without much of a hand in the hope that your opponent shows weakness and you can bluff him/her later

To Open/Opening the action – First to act

Peeling – Calling with the hope of hitting a card in the future to make your hand

Playing The Board – You are relying solely on the board and not your hole cards

Rabbit Hunting – When players check undealt cards e.g. if a hand finishes before all cards have been dealt

Shove – Moving all-in

Squeeze play – Typically a large raise after one player has opened and several have called

Three-bet/Four-bet/Five-bet – Reraise/re-reraise/re-re-reraise!

Value bet – A bet that you believe will get called more often than not by a worse hand

Cards/Hands/Pots

Backdoor – In conjunction with 'draw', 'straight' or 'flush' – when a player has three cards to a flush or a straight on the flop, and hits two cards in a row to get there

Broadway – A-K-Q-J-10. Can also refer to cards within that group

Family pot – All or almost all players call during the first round of betting

Kicker – The deciding card between tied hands

Rag – Card of little value

Runner-runner – Two cards needed to make a hand that come one after the other

Scare card – A card that is likely to improve an opponent's hand

chapter 4

Psychology & Strategy

Introducing strategy

You may have started playing poker because you saw your flatmates at it one night and thought you could give them a run for their money; perhaps your boss has decided that this year they are going to have a Christmas poker event instead of a party (born from a night he watched Rounders and now thinks he's Matt Damon), or you may just want to fleece your Grandmother at the family get-together; whatever the reason – putting a little time into thinking about the game will not only help to improve the outcome, but also teach you a lot about yourself and others.

I understand that not everyone reading this book is expecting to chuck in their job in the morning and hit the live poker circuit, armed only with a toothbrush and a dream. But whatever the reason you want to play, why not give yourself the best shot to win and see how good you can be? In doing so, you will learn skills that can be transferred to many other aspects of life. Trust me, there are poker faces (and not so good poker faces) everywhere – from the boardroom to the dating scene.

Poker is a game of mathematics, guts, observation, instinct, psychology, patience and discipline; so it goes without saying that there is a lot to think about when it comes to strategy and finding what works for you. When starting out, there is some basic strategy you can apply, though. Sticking to the top range of starting hands (your hole cards) is a good tool and will help you play more confidently, even in more vulnerable positions. The strongest starting hands are A-A, K-K, Q-Q and A-Ks (s is for suited i.e. matching suits). Note: don't be too star-struck if you find yourself with 'pocket rockets' (A-A), the 'ladies' (Q-Q) or the 'big slick' (A-K), if you have a few people prepared to call during a game, then you are going to have to think about what they are calling with and also adapt to what comes on the board. For instance, you find a couple of 'cowboys' (K-K) in your hand and a few players call your raise to see a flop that features an ace. Don't get too married to your hand, remember any ace will beat you right here.

If you wait solely to play the cream of the crop, you might be waiting a while, in fact, you may end up losing a chunk of chips to the blinds because monster hands do not come around too often. Let's widen the choice with some more starting hands: A-Qs; J-J; K-Qs; and A-Js. When you get more comfortable and have a little more experience under your belt, you can start looking at playing even more hands, such as other pairs and suited connectors (hands that are connected and of the same suit e.g. 10 of hearts and 9 of hearts).

If you're playing with medium to small pairs (as your hole cards), you're usually just set 'mining' i.e. hunting down that third card to make a set. So don't go reaching for the chips and smiling like a Cheshire cat when you see two nines in your hand – think about where you are at the table, who is next to act, if you should bet, what you're willing to call for the chance to hit, and what your plan is if you don't. A useful way to learn more about hands and probability is by using a poker odds calculator. There are many free versions online that you can play around with.

Knowing which hands are the best to play and exactly when to play them is a great starting point for any player. It's kind of like learning enough chords to get you through some beginner guitar tracks. This is a nice step towards that wickedly wild guitar solo you know is in you bursting to get out.

The mathematics of poker

For many players, poker is all about mathematics. For others, it's just one corner of the web they use to trap their prey. Either way, it's extremely important if you want to make the best decisions you can at the table.

When playing, you have a lot to keep an eye out for and that includes the chip stacks around you. You should always be aware of the size of the chip stacks your opponents have as this is the ammunition they are going to use against you. You should be counting up their stacks and yours regularly to see where you stand among them. This information will affect how you utilise your own stack. Look for the short stacks; look for where all the chips are; see how the blinds are affecting your stack; and where you stand in the greater scheme of things with the overall chip average. Now let's move on from eyeballing your opponents' chips to find out how mathematics can be used to enhance, and often determine, your success rate when in combat at the table.

Poker player, writer, producer and coach Gareth Chantler shares some basic thoughts on the mathematics of poker. Quick note: Gareth uses a popular form of hand reporting you will find throughout this book. This sees cards described by rank followed by suit. (Example: Kh is King of hearts and 2s is the 2 of spades). Contrary to most people's gut reaction, when it comes to poker, math doesn't have to be a four-letter word. In poker the essential mathematics is mercifully straightforward.

Pot Odds

Your opponent bets the size of the pot on the river and you are thinking of calling, but aren't sure if you should. This is one of poker's most familiar, and difficult, situations. But the mathematics is easy. How often do you need to win after calling to make money? The answer is more than one third of the time. How do we know? Well you have to pay the bet to win the bet and the pot. And the bet is equal to the size of the pot. So you have to pay one pot-sized bet to win two of them.

When you win, you pick up those two. When you lose, you surrender your one. That means you can lose twice as often as you win and still break even. If are winning more often than that, you're laughing. Well making money that is; you probably shouldn't laugh while you rake in other people's money.

...now with numbers!

If you can smile and nod through the above example you are well on your way to grasping the math of this game. And if you notice above, there are no symbols, no long division, and no differential equations.

It is risk (pot) versus reward (pot plus pot).

Let's use some numbers to make things a bit more concrete.

If there is $100 in the pot and our opponent bets $100, we have to call $100 to win $200. As we've already solved, we need to win at least one third of the time to put our money down.

But what if our opponent bets, say, $50? What does our proposition look like now?

Well we are going to have to risk $50 now to win $150, instead of $100 for $200. It turns out we have to win less often to make money. We are risking 1 to win 3. So we can lose three $50 calls for every time we scoop up the $150, and still break even.

So now we need to win one quarter of the time, 25%, or more. Win more often than that and you're laughing (but in your head this time).

Equity and outs

Equity

Equity sure looks like a big word for just six-letters. Fear not! We looked at two examples on the previous page where we faced a decision on the river, when there were no more cards to come. Well, what if there are cards to come? What does math have to say for itself then?

In poker, equity is just a fancy way of saying chance of winning. So for example, some bespectacled fancy-pants will say, 'before the flop, A-K's equity against pocket queens ('pocket' meaning matching hole cards) is 44%.' That means A-K has a 44% chance of winning against queens if we were to deal out the five community cards.

So let's go back to our previous examples:

If we have A-K and have to call $50 to win a potential $150 pot, we have to win 25% of the time, right? We figured that out already (see the previous page if you're unsure). So if there are five-cards to come, we can imagine that we're almost definitely going to be making money calling $50 to win $150 with A-K.

Even if our opponent turns over pocket kings, we have enough chance of winning (equity) that a call would earn us money and folding would leave money on the table. This is because our chances to win against pocket kings, with A-K, are closer to 30%. Those pot-odds work regardless of where you are in a hand. Count the bet. Count the pot. Compare. The mathematics stays the same. One of the hardest parts of the game is evaluating how good or bad the next card to come off the deck will be for you. But the river is in some ways the simplest part of the game – there is no longer any chance of a hand's strength changing. You don't need to look into the future anymore. On the river, you either have the best hand or you don't.

Psychology & Strategy

Thankfully, we can practice looking up our chance of winning, like learning new words from the dictionary. As exciting as that sounds, there are some shortcuts too. For example, a higher pocket pair versus a smaller pocket pair is an 80% to 20% proposition before the flop.

Outs

Outs are cards that, generally speaking, will give you the best hand, if you don't already have it. Sometimes outs are clear, like if you need a heart to fall to complete your flush. However, sometimes those outs are a bit murkier, like if you're looking for an ace or a king when you're holding A-K on a ten-high board. If, in this case, your opponent has two kings, then two kings have gone from the deck that you were counting on for help. The more cards you count that could be available to improve your hand, the better. Therefore the more outs you count, the more comfortable you should feel in a hand. There are some short-cuts for calculating the chance of winning, by counting one's outs. Let's look at some helpful examples:

(Before the flop):

71.4% for Kc-Ks versus 28.6% for As-Qh

52.5% for Jh-Th versus 47.5% for 5c-5s

59.5% Ac-Ts versus 49.5% for Ks-Qh

(On a 7c-5c-2c flop):

49.6% for Ac-Ks versus 50.40% for 8c-8s

33.4% for 5s-5h versus 66.6% for Ac-4c

(On a 9c-8c-4s-2c turn):

38.6% for Q-J versus 61.4% for Ah-9h

90.9% for Qc-Tc versus 9.1% for 9d-8d

You are never going to be able to know your exact chance of winning in any given situation because you will never know your opponent's exact cards (unless you have say Q-Q on a Q-Q-4-2 board – pretty sure you'll win that one). Know what your price is and then do your best estimating. Knowing the range of different hands your opponent could have – well that's a bit harder!

Tells

Good poker players will always be on the lookout for information wherever and whenever they can get it. You can get a ton of information about your opponents from what they do and how they do it simply by watching for behaviour and changes in that behaviour. These pieces of information that are there for the taking are known as 'reads' or 'tells' and they come from what a player says and does, as well as their betting patterns.

This is where paying attention to what is happening around you comes in handy. Certain tells manifest themselves through noticeable physical changes and are certainly not deliberate – for example a blotchy neck, shaky hands, eye movements, changes in breathing, nervous twitches, or perhaps via speech play (when a player attempts to convince or manipulate his or her opponent one way or another). These kind of tells often occur when players try to conceal, or act the opposite of, what they are feeling. I remember intently reading (Mike) *Caro's Book of Tells – The Psychology and Body Language of Poker*; this book had a remarkable effect on me, as all of a sudden I found myself routinely analysing the body language of not only players, but my colleagues, my friends, as well as strangers, like that cocky guy in front of me. Mannerisms and behaviour will either spell weakness or strength, purposely or unconsciously, and generally poker players will try to come across as strong when they are weak, and weak when they are strong.

When you make a move at the poker table, you are looking for a particular reaction. The same goes for your opponents. If you can work out what it is they really want you to do and do the opposite, you'll stay ahead of the pack. To do this you need to look out for patterns and breaks in patterns. If you can tie different actions and reactions to when a player is strong and when they are weak, then you are building information up about this person that may help you in future hands.

For me, this intense human element is just another reason to love poker. We make mistakes, we're not always the best actors, and our bodies often give us away. At the poker table, there really is nowhere to hide. That's why you might find players wearing scarves, sunglasses, hats, hoodies or all of the above. They don't want you to see when they don't have it, but they also don't want you to see when they do! A good poker player does not need any of that get-up in my opinion. A good poker player should act the same when they are strong as when they are weak (unless they are of Academy-award winning acting quality) plus their betting patterns will not give any unnecessary details away.

There is an abundance of useful information out there about body language and poker tells. If you can apply this to your experience and observations of your opponents, you will have yet another weapon at your disposal at the poker table.

Remember, information is key. Your job is to get hold of as much of it as you can and then turn it to your advantage.

Psychology & Strategy

The art of bluffing

We've all done it in our lives. Whether it's in work, with friends, with our other halves; there comes a time when a little white lie is needed, maybe a little faking?

'Have you got that report, Rebecca?'. 'Oh yes, I'm right on top of it – it should be done soon!' warrants a better response than 'No, I haven't had time. I'm far too busy and if you stress me out more I'm gonna...'

What about when you really liked someone but you deliberately didn't respond to them for a whole, painful day just to pretend like it wasn't the most important thing in your world right then. Or when you were meant to go to that thing but simply didn't want to, so you 'pulled a sickie'.

People play these games sometimes to help them to deal with situations better; to keep people away, to draw them in, to make something seem better than it is, to make something seem worse than it is, to fool someone into wanting something they didn't realise they wanted before... this kind of psychological warfare happens every day.

A sprinkle of this isn't harmful, especially if it's not hurting anyone. And if it's done right, the desired result or effect can be achieved. However, if done too much, it has the opposite effect. No one will believe you whether you're telling the truth or not, people will expect you to be playing games with them, and ultimately, people will lose respect for what you say and do. This is bluffing. An art that, in my opinion, needs balance and practice – this is true in both life and poker.

In the preconceptions section I mentioned that there is the misapprehension that women don't bluff – that they play too 'tight' and conservatively to do that. Then you have those of the opinion that 'women are not to be trusted'. The benefit of this conflict is that you can be a relatively unknown quantity at the table, with the power to tell any story you like.

A bluff doesn't have to mean taking a big chance or involving yourself in an outrageous gamble. A true bluff (for want of a better word) should be calculated, strategic and seamless. When the best bluffs work, they are surprising, bewildering even, and always impressive. They work because they make sense – so they are believable.

To the outside world a bluffer might sound like your ol' uncle Bob who will play any game the same – a master concealer, manipulator, gambler, and charmer who rarely has anything to show for his claims. In poker, bluffing doesn't simply mean making a move with nothing to back it up. It is an art, and it takes a heavy dose of concentration and observation to pull it off. It involves strategic decision-making, based on strong perception and skill.

And it might all happen in mere minutes, maybe even seconds. Over time, you will learn how to use your image, how important your position at the table is, and when to get involved with, how should I put it, less desirable starting hands. It doesn't always matter what's in your hands, the important tool you need to beat your opponent, is information.

To bluff successfully and indeed to prevent being bluffed, you need to learn how to spot weakness and recognise what does not make sense. But this comes after being in similar situations again and again and seeing repeats of the same actions and reactions. It also comes from making mistakes and finding out the hard way. Practise will ensure better recognition of a good opportunity to bluff. But to take advantage of such an opportunity you must be willing to go with your calculations, your instinct, and your observations.

You want to be the one who pulls the Ocean's 11-type con, not one of the world's worst robbers caught on tape.

When you make a weak, unplanned, uncalculated bluff and it happens to come through for you, all that is to be felt is relief. Sometimes a little embarrassment. You should rarely be saying to yourself, 'I can't believe I got away with that.' When a strong, well-thought-out bluff works out, all you want to do is pat

yourself on the back. You added everything up, made a decision and you were right. Admittedly, there is perhaps always a sense of relief as there rarely is 100 per cent certainty in any given situation.

I used to find getting caught bluffing very embarrassing, but even a good bluff doesn't always work out. It's less embarrassing when the revealed bluff is intelligent and rational but can also make your opponent look like an absolute hero – they smelled the very clever rat and exposed it.

You will make mistakes. Your judgment, your timing, your instincts may not always be on point. But you must be willing to sharpen your skills so that you are not just relying on the two cards in your hands. Just because a bluff is called doesn't make it bad. Bluffing is essential to getting paid with value bets against good observant players who may notice you haven't been bluffing. You shouldn't bluff curious players, however, as it will rarely work.

I should also add that there comes a time where you may have a great hand, but you feel like due to timing or the image you have cultivated at the table that the only way to perhaps get some value for it is to look like you're bluffing and/or playing scared. In my opinion this is the only time you should be bluffing scared – Academy Award-nominee kinda scared!

When concealing a big hand or making a ballsy play with just the thought that your opponent is too weak to call, your heart will probably feel like it's going to come right out of your chest. Your breathing may alter, your skin can redden, you may find yourself fidgeting, or it might become difficult to speak. If all of a sudden you're acting differently to how you had before, a good opponent will recognise this in an instant. Now you could be lucky and they could be so weak this won't matter, but this is something you have to learn to control or conceal. What I've learned is to act the same whatever I have in my hand. If you're talkative, stay talkative. If you're quiet, stay quiet. Or how about every time you get into an intense situation you stare at a certain spot and don't respond. Whatever works for you, do it, but do it every time.

Using your femininity

Using one's femininity at the poker table can have various meanings. It can be using the perceptions of female players to your advantage, manipulating your relationship with different types of male players, or even flirting and using physical assets as a distraction or lure. I would rather steer clear of the latter, but how you play is totally up to you.

If we as women are playing solely on the idea that we're seen a certain way, then this is not always going to work out so well. Aside from manipulation of gender perception, to be successful in the long-term, we must develop many other skills and ensure we adjust our game as the attitudes of those around us (hopefully) change.

It's confusing; we can talk about sexism in life, in the workplace, or in poker, but then at the same time use gender-based attributes and perceptions to succeed. However, poker is about information; it's about what we know about the here and now, and how we can use every detail. Any good player will use whatever edge they can to get ahead, so if this means using current thoughts about your play to your advantage, then that is just one tool we have at our disposal right now. Professional poker player Katie Stone says, 'Playing like a girl is wonderful. To me, it means being smart and utilizing all my tools to win. It means that I have an advantage over everyone, because I know that I am always going to be initially regarded as weak. This is more information that I have, that my opponents do not have. My edge is immediate for me as soon as I sit down.'

Fatima de Melo stands out at a poker table. She is not only talented but has presence and charisma. She says she loves playing amongst men. 'They're so easy-going most of the time and usually a little surprised when I get involved in the "changing room" talk at the table. I'm not what they seem to expect from a small, blonde girl,' she says. 'On the poker level it's good to know that most male players see female players as being really tight players, so I like to play that card, especially in the first couple levels of a tournament... and then pick my spots to bluff later on when the blinds have gone up.'

Your physical presence at a live poker table is always going to provoke a certain response whether you're a man or woman. After all, a large part of poker is trying to figure out the kind of player your opponent is, and their strengths and weaknesses, based on any information you have at your disposal. I wrote a thesis in college about women in poker and in it I explored some of the different types of men you will meet at the poker table and how they can treat you and play against you. They fell into roles like the mentor, the bully, the flirt, and each had their own approach. I spoke with Melanie Weisner about using femininity at the poker table and discovered these characters certainly did still exist. This is what she had to say:

'Presence at the poker table is one of the most valuable assets you have as a player, and one of the most under-utilized. This can be exploited from many different aspects, not just as a female – age, dress, attitude, and behaviour has just as much associated stereotype and particulars that a

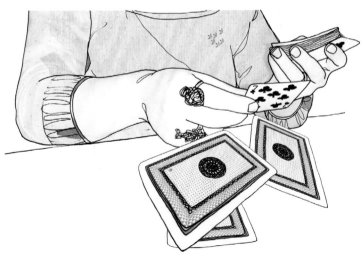

smart player will be able to use to their advantage. Being a female at the poker table presents a very strong advantage.

As a female, I have experienced distinct advantages in a myriad of ways. At a very base level, men often enjoy having a pretty lady at the table. It breaks up the monotony of a bunch of testosterone at battle over cards. Often, men will 'soft-play' women at the table, which is defined by them not extracting as much value as they could out of their hands, in order to save you from losing too much. It is quite easy to spot this type of player, and often they will even tell you something like, 'I'm only betting XX to save you from losing too much.' (But always be wary of table talk!) Then there is the opposite end of the spectrum – a palpable discomfort playing hands with a woman. This can be for a few reasons - they can feel psychologically out of their element, or they can simply feel uncomfortable since it is rare for men to get involved in battle with women at the table. These types of players will often play one way versus the other players at their table, and a different way against you. Many times, I have experienced a seemingly solid, tight player going berserk or playing distinctly erratically versus me, and visibly being uncomfortable. You will notice this type of behaviour if you see elements in their play against you that doesn't match up to what you've seen versus the rest of the table.

The third, and most common, type of way that men adjust to women at the table is by either giving you too much credit (they will be willing to make big laydowns to you, and view you as being very tight as is stereotypical for a female), or they will not give you enough credit (they will be trying to run you over at every opportunity since they view you as weak). The

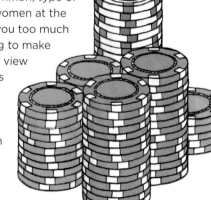

first way is much easier to play against, but there are clear ways to combat the second type of player – be more selective about hands you play, as weak hands' profitability will diminish versus a player with this type of aggression, but be willing to be more forceful with your stronger hands and don't be scared off them.

Women seemed to be more naturally attuned to psychological factors at play in-game than men do, probably because of generally more intricate senses of social behaviour and an ability to manipulate those factors with more ease and subtlety (there are, of course, very smart men who are adept at using these types of psychological elements to their advantage). To begin with, I recommend utilizing speech to try to gain information from your opponents. If you can engage them in conversation, before or during play, you will find yourself having a much better idea of where you stand and what a player is capable of and willing to do when against you, which is a valuable asset.

The ideal situation is for you to be able to command the different ways your feminine presence can be advantageous, and be able to then execute whichever suits the situation correctly. You should be able to pick out players that will soft-play you, and ask to see their hands if you plan on making a big fold to them. You should be able to spot the players that are going to give you a lot of credit, and pick good bluff spots against these players. You should be able to more freely hero-call players that want to try to run you over, and you should be able to pick up on subtle social and psychological factors at play - both involving you and other players at the table - and use those to more accurately determine how likely it is that a player can be manipulated to your desired action. Lastly, you should be able to not only respond to all the ways your opponents will naturally behave towards you, but become adept at specifically manipulating your own image to elicit these types of reactions, in whichever direction you deem most profitable for the situation.'

chapter 5

Playing Live

Entering the real world

There are only a few things in the world that make me feel as alive and excited as I do when I sit down to play at the live felt. The decisions I make are entirely my own, I have the chance to test myself and strengthen my awareness of different situations and people, how I experience what I'm about to experience is, in most part, up to me, and the potential is there for anything to happen.

I think a positive approach goes a long way, as does a good sleep the night before an event, plus a healthy breakfast or lunch. I force myself to do this because eating and sleeping is the last thing I want to do when I know I'll soon be sitting down to play. These days I don't get to play as much, working in the industry. So when I do, I'm like a kid at Christmas. This is obviously something I have to control because information like that could be used against me. Knowing how little I get to play now and how much it means when I do could make some players think I'll be playing tight or more conservatively than usual, not wanting to go home too early. Damn, did I let the cat out of the bag? Nope! If I put the money down to play then I have to be willing to lose it. For me, the fun, lessons learned and time spent is always worth it anyway.

I recently introduced someone to their first live event and he could not get over the sound of the chips riffling in unison throughout the room. 'It sounds like rain!' he said in disbelief. And it does. A sea of people clinking their chips, trying to play their A game, hoping to go home in profit. Walk into a major live event and you'll feel the buzz immediately. You may find that not everyone there will be open to chatting or having a laugh, but I have never left a tournament without a funny story or a new friend.

What you wear and how you present yourself at the table can say different things about you. I have known a few female players who have tried out different looks to see how they work and what the response is in live poker. The different reactions you can get when you pay more or less attention to your appearance is really quite amazing. You are not more or less serious about the game depending on what outfit you put on, but people do like their stereotypes. Fortunately, this can be to their detriment.

My advice for a beginner is to just be comfortable and be yourself. Oh and bring something warm to throw on – air conditioning can be very distracting! You may be sitting there for a while so those pants that cut off circulation after 10 minutes are definitely a no-no. I always like it when people make an effort, especially in live events. I don't believe that female players should dress with their male opponents in mind – there's a lot more to think about than how we look. I do, however, believe all players should respect the game in the ways in which they behave and present themselves.

Playing live poker will certainly help you develop skills in observation, confidence and self-control. It can help you separate fact from emotional thought while also teach you lessons in intuition and self-belief. There may be many things you didn't realise about yourself until you sat down at a poker table. So what other areas of your life can benefit from this new-found knowledge? The skills you learn or strengthen at the live felt are skills you will take with you throughout your entire life.

Playing Live

Tackling a live tournament

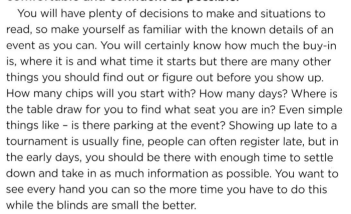

It's not too hard to spot a beginner at a table so you should do what you can to make yourself as comfortable and confident as possible.

You will have plenty of decisions to make and situations to read, so make yourself as familiar with the known details of an event as you can. You will certainly know how much the buy-in is, where it is and what time it starts but there are many other things you should find out or figure out before you show up. How many chips will you start with? How many days? Where is the table draw for you to find what seat you are in? Even simple things like – is there parking at the event? Showing up late to a tournament is usually fine, people can often register late, but in the early days, you should be there with enough time to settle down and take in as much information as possible. You want to see every hand you can so the more time you have to do this while the blinds are small the better.

Most tournaments see blinds start small and increase every level. The amount and frequency just depends on the structure of the event you're playing. For instance perhaps the blinds start at 25/50 and increase every 30 minutes. This means the small blind is 25 and the big blind is 50 and this will change to 50 and 100 after 30 minutes.

Blind levels typically increase as a tournament progresses. At a certain level, players will often be hit with an 'ante'. An ante is a small compulsory bet to be made by all players on the table before the cards are dealt. As the levels change, so do the chips. Higher value chips make an appearance while the lower value ones are taken away – this is known as 'colouring up' or a 'chip race'.

The amount of players taking part in an event normally determines how much the prize pool is, as each buy-in goes into a central pot. Sometimes sponsors will add to the prize pool or guarantee a certain amount. The prize structure and payouts are decided when registration for the event closes. Not everyone will be paid, so if you bust out before the payouts you will go home with nothing. If you are the last to bust before the money then this is known as the 'bubble'. Play usually slows up around the bubble as no-one wants to go home so close to the money. The more professional players get active and take advantage by being more aggressive because amateurs or weaker players are more inclined to be passive and tight.

Events will usually have a small break after a couple of levels and then a big break later in the day for dinner. The final table usually comprises eight or nine players – it just depends on the event format and what has previously been decided. Sometimes the remaining players make a deal and this can occur at any time but mostly at the final table. When there are just two players left this is known as 'heads up'. This format is not the same as playing with other players at the table. You are always in the action, always in the blinds, and always have a decision to make. You can't just sit and wait for a better hand; you have to work with what you're given. There are heads-up events you can play online and live, in order to practise this element of your game.

Event information is key especially while an event is running – in bigger tournaments this may be on screens around the room, but in local or pub events, you might just have to holler! Information is everything in poker and there should be plenty of it all around you. At any given time you should be aware of how much the blinds are, how many chips you have in relation to this (how many big blinds you have in total), what the average chip stack is, and roughly what those around you have. Knowing the structure of the event you're playing and paying attention to the details around you will give you vital information you can use to your advantage. Let's focus on what you know for sure and then start working on the variables - this will give you a good start and make you feel more confident in your new adventure.

Over the years I've asked many professionals what it is they love about being a poker player. Nine times out of ten the answer is the same – freedom. They can do what they like, when they like, how they like with who they like. They control their own schedules, bankroll, and travel plans and can go on crazy adventures when and where they wish. This, it should be said, would all end pretty quickly without the bankroll management part. Those without sponsorship cannot just go jetting off to every live event, and successful poker players need to think about the cost of living in whatever city it may be, on top of travel expenses and the money needed to play. Qualifying online or live is generally a good way to go. You spend a small amount to play for a live event ticket so you don't have to spend a chunk of cash buying in directly. Those who last in the industry are those who treat poker as a job and show discipline when it comes to the game and the life it can bring. You won't see them splashing the cash in the local nightclub and turning up to play after one hour's sleep. They give themselves the best possible chance to win.

When talking about what she loves about the game, Team PokerStars Pro player, and hockey star, Fatima Moreira de Melo says, 'I feel so independent and so lucky to be able to travel to play the game I love! I've also met a lot of interesting individuals, people who dare to follow a different path than most. I love alternative thinkers and you'll find a lot of them in the poker world.' Whatever you do in the poker world, you will meet a huge amount of characters and you will have an unbelievable amount of stories to bring home.

Poker has brought me to some of the most incredible places in the world and given me unforgettable experiences. There is so much fun to be had on and off the felt, and whether working or playing you will find people from all ages, races, genders, and backgrounds interacting regardless of language. Professional poker pro Xuan Liu says, 'I've always wanted to travel the world since I was quite young, and poker has given me opportunities and adventures beyond my imagination. Everybody wants to be a rock star, but most don't have the musical talent. Poker is a way for introverts, nerds, and dreamers to experience that kind of lifestyle.'

No matter where you are, it should not be too hard to find live poker close by. Apart from local clubs and events, there is the World Poker Tour, European Poker Tour, Asia Pacific Poker Tour and Aussie Millions

to name but a few, plus oodles of regional tours. For me, the live poker world is much like a traveling circus. Tours pull into town, set up, and open their doors. Then in come the masses – the same familiar faces, plus a whole load of strangers who have yet to become friends. The air is thick with excitement. This is where lessons are learned and shared. This is where fascinating stories begin and end. This is where dreams are dashed but for some, they can and will come true.

Etiquette

Just like in any sport or game, in poker there are many rules. These cover a variety of scenarios, protecting both the players and the game. In the past there were players who made a name for themselves for being cocky or argumentative at the table but generally poor sportsmanship is frowned upon and unnecessary. Having good poker etiquette doesn't mean having to dilute your personality or style of play, it just means having respect for those around you, the tournament staff, and the game in general. There are a few things you should know especially as a beginner.

Let's start with the dealer. These amazing people have to put up with every kind of person there is out there. You should always try to make their job as easy as possible. It really doesn't take much to be polite. The cards they deal you are random, they are NOT a reflection of what they think of you and they are NOT doing anything on purpose. Tipping when playing live cash games and/or when you have a good score in a tournament is advised.

Next on the list is paying attention to when it's your turn to act. It's fine to have a chat or a look around but you should not let the players around you or the dealer have to wait each time the action comes back to you. This can get old, really quickly! On that note, acting out of turn can be just as bad and can result in penalties (like having to sit out for a few hands). Acting out of turn does not just impact you, it can have a domino effect and give information away or spoil someone else's plan. People make mistakes, but the more you focus on what's happening around you, the fewer mistakes you will make.

Put your blinds out when it's your turn and antes (see previous page) out when they kick in. With antes, just try to remember that you're putting an amount in before every hand. I say try because I'm a bit of a culprit for forgetting.

Playing Live

It's sensible to ensure that no-one has to remind you of the things you really should be paying attention to, so make a mental note to stay focused. You will soon learn it's not as easy as it sounds – that's why playing poker can be so tiring!

Another thing new players tend to do is misplace their bets or splash the pot – you should put your bet over the line in front of you in one motion and then the dealer will bring the bets together into one pot once the betting round is complete. If you put your bet straight into the pot this can get confusing for everyone. If you throw your chips in front of you, it won't be clear what exactly you have done. If you intend to bet and don't place your chips over the line in one motion but allow them to fall as they may, then only the minimum amount will be counted (this is called 'string betting'). My advice is take your time when deciding what to do and then act. It also helps to state what you are doing. For instance, if someone has bet and you intend to raise but just put out one large denomination chip in front of you, it can be counted as a call. If you announce 'raise', then no-one can question your action. You don't have to announce everything, you can also use actions to speak for you. As an alternative to saying 'check' you can knock or tap on the table and if you don't want to say 'fold' then just muck your cards. However, until you get comfortable with the flow of the game, stating what you're doing can prevent any misunderstandings.

There are many things I have seen at the poker table that make me want to stand up and yell. These are not just performed by beginners. In fact, it would be understandable if they were. Here's a shortened list of what not to do at a poker table.

- Rub it in when you beat someone. Be courteous – the act of winning the hand is more than enough. Do not over celebrate.
- If it's you and your opponent and you are going to raise an amount that would essentially put their tournament life at risk if they were to call, then don't say, 'I'll put you all-in'. It's more polite to simply raise an amount that puts the other person at risk than to be so direct. Remember they have the choice to fold so you can't make them move all-in.
- Don't put your phone on the table or take a call – this is normally not allowed anyway.
- Don't talk loudly while other players are in a hand – you'll understand why when someone does it to you.
- Don't talk about a hand you're not involved in.
- Respect the time people take to make decisions.
- If you call and your opponent shows their cards and you are beaten, you don't have to show your hand unless asked to. Asking to see someone's mucked cards doesn't happen frequently as it is considered to be a bit rude. This one often depends on where you're playing.
- If you're not sure if you have won or not, just show your hand. Being tentative in turning over when you're unsure can look like a slow roll if you in fact have the winning hand. A slow roll is when you deliberately take your time in turning your cards over when your hand is the best. No one likes a slow roller!
- Do not show your neighbour, or anyone your cards, during or after a hand. The rule is generally – show one, show all. If you do show one, be prepared that someone will catch you and force you to show the entire table. Showing cards is generally not a good thing to do. Remember what I said about giving away information?

This one is more of a poker rule than etiquette but gets kind of annoying when you see someone complaining about it, so it's going in here:

- Protect your hand – the dealer will swipe your cards away if it looks like you're not using them. Put a chip or a card protector on top and keep them close-by on the table. That way, no one can touch 'em!

Tips for beginners

I recently asked professional poker player Ben Jenkins to show some people I work with how to play poker and teach them tips on how to be successful early on in their poker journey. As they bounded out into the world ready to take on all-comers I thought that his advice would be perfect in preparing you for your time at the felt. Here are the wonderful Ben Jenkins' tips:

Playing Live

Keep things simple

Poker can be a complicated game, but it doesn't need to be. It's possible to make your decisions in a way that will make potential future decisions easier. I always advise beginners to be mindful of this.

For example, you're playing No Limit Hold 'em and have Q-Q, there is $13,450 in the pot and the community cards read Jh 7c 6h Qc. You are first to act with 10,500 chips in your current stack and two opponents still in the pot. While you have the best hand possible right now, there are many possible hands your opponent can have that can outdraw you. I see a lot of people trying to keep their opponents in the pot in this spot, betting around $4,000–$6000, only for a card to roll off on the river leaving a tricky situation where your opponent has likely made a flush or straight. Instead I'd recommend moving all-in on the turn – the pot is already quite big and most hands your opponents could have are draws, since there is only one queen left, and a lower set or two pair probably won't fold. In any case we don't want cards to fall that stop these hands paying you off for the maximum! Sometimes your opponents will want to gamble with their draw too, or believe you are trying to push them off a hand with a draw yourself and call with a weak hand that is drawing dead to your top set. Either way you eliminate any tricky guess-work you may have had to make on the river. By keeping the pot simple for yourself you have ensured that you can't make a mistake, and in poker you largely profit by forcing opponents into mistakes.

Play the good hands!

Pairs, big aces and suited broadways (10-J, J-Q, Q-K or K-A belonging to the same suit) are the best hands because they hit the flop the most often, making the strongest hands – sets, top pairs, straights and flushes. Making the best hands is going to make you a favourite to win the pots while also making the game easier. If you find yourself making a second and third pair a lot, you can end up in a lot of tricky spots and we're trying to keep it simple.

Play your hands in position

When you have the button or are to the right of it (the 'cut-off'), then you are going to be able to watch the action before making your decision. Poker is a game of incomplete information, but by trying to play most of our hands 'in position' - that is last to act – we have much more information than everybody has had to act before us. The more information

you have the easier it will be to make a good decision and avoid a mistake. Be very selective about what hands you play from early position where the positional disadvantage is the most acute. You want hands that will remain strong once the flop is dealt – typically big pairs and aces – and to actively look for opportunities in which to aggressively press any positional advantage you may have. In late position, typically the button and cut off, small pairs and suited connectors become much more playable – although not from a shallow stack as you need enough chips behind to realise the implied odds of these hands (taking into consideration future betting) when you do hit a good flop.

Playing live

Online poker is a great way to get into poker – you can play
a lot of hands quickly from the confines of your own home
without worrying about giving any tells away. However, many
people also enjoy playing live where you get to meet, and
chat to, many different opponents. People often remark that
they find some of the aspects of live poker quite daunting;
they are worried about giving away tells, muddling around
with chips or acting out of turn. Largely I think these fears
are unfounded if you take your time, breathe and remain

calm, follow the action and concentrate on other people, how they are acting, and how they play their hands. You'll be too busy to worry about giving off tells yourself, but if you think you are, then find a routine and do the same things every hand. Don't be the player holding their cards to fold before it's your turn, look at your cards and place your hands on the table the same way each time. If you aren't comfortable handling chips, don't play around with them, and when making bets, announce them to the dealer and use the largest chips you have. If ever you are unsure of the action, for example who is next to act, then ask the dealer. Remember, in poker we are simply trying to avoid mistakes. Also, take the time to get to meet your table mates. There are many interesting people that play poker – it's a very social game. Relax and enjoy it.

Ultimately, nothing is more valuable than experience in poker. After seeing the same situation repeatedly, if you are paying attention, you will begin to instinctively know what's going on. You will begin to interpret the information you gather at the table more accurately, such as people's betting patterns or the way they handle their chips or hold their cards, which will lead you to make better decisions.

There is a lot to be said for good strong logic in poker, so take your time, think things through, have a plan and be consistent. I love the challenges the game presents to me. I've played for over ten years but am still constantly learning and evolving the way I think about the game. Be reflective; if you aren't sure about a hand you have played, don't be shy to ask a more experienced player what they think. Not everybody plays the same, and there is not usually one right course of action, but it never hurts to take on board other people's opinions. Most of all though, have fun, nothing else will keep you motivated to improve more, and of course, it never hurts to be lucky once in a while.

chapter 6

Playing Online

Log on, log in and play

Although online poker means you don't have that physical or even emotional interaction with your opponents, there is a lot to be learned about your game from playing on the virtual felt. Online poker rooms, and indeed mobile poker applications, make it possible to play more poker, more frequently. This rapidly increases the number of hands you can play, so you can learn about your game at a much quicker rate than you would live. You can also make notes about your online opponents so if you run into them again you have information about them, plus you can analyse your hand histories post-play and/or make use of software developed to help players better track and understand their play online.

There are numerous online poker rooms you can try out until you find one, or even a few, you are comfortable with, and there are usually very good first depositor's bonuses to be found if you shop around. You can play very cheaply online and even for free in tournaments called 'Freerolls'. This means you don't have to pay to play the tournament, but you could win money or online tickets if you get into the payouts. You usually have to beat out a high number of players to do so, but it's good experience and fun!

There are a wide range of stakes, games and formats online and no matter what the time of day is, you will always find a seat. Something quite exciting about online poker is the amount of satellites. Satellites are tournaments where the goal is to win a seat into a bigger event, either online or live. Satellites also give players a cheap way to qualify for a variety of live events held all around the world, from the comfort of their own sitting rooms. For the price of a take-away or less, live event satellite winners get a free pass to Main Event buy-ins worth thousands as well as expenses towards flights, and luxury accommodation. Then, when qualifiers go to this city

or place to play the Main
Event, they have a shot at an
even bigger prize pool. So you
could start out playing for a live
package in your pyjamas sitting in
bed, and end up in the Bahamas in
your bikini with a shot at hundreds of
thousands of dollars!

There are many female players making a living and more
from their online play. Recent data analysis of two online
tournament series, the PokerStars Micro Millions 6 and the
2012 World Championship of Online Poker, indicated that
there was not a significant difference between the results of
female and male poker players. In fact, the data showed that
male players played more events on average, therefore
further research may show that women were in fact more
successful overall in this particular study. The number of
women playing online is growing, so it's only a matter of time
before that growth becomes more visible in the live realm.

My main tip here for beginners would be to make sure you
treat online poker as you would live poker and stay focused
on what's going on. Do not rely on the timer's buzzer going
off to remind you it's your turn or that you're even playing;
so turn off the TV or whatever else is in front of you that is
making you miss vital information. Just because you're not
in a hand doesn't mean it's time to check Facebook!

How online poker works

You know when you come home from work on a Friday night and make the big mistake of taking off your shoes and sitting down on the couch? You were meant to meet some friends but the possibility of you venturing outside slips ever so quickly out of reach as you sink further into the warmth of the leather. Long gone are the days you needed to leave the house for a game if you felt like playing but weren't in the mood to face the world. Aside from the practical benefits online poker brought to those who already played for a living, the ability to play using the internet made things so easy if slouching around in your PJs was your choice du jour or if you only had a few hours to spare.

Playing Online

There is no doubting the many benefits to playing online – we'll talk about that shortly – but first let's look at how online poker works. The best way to understand it is to give it a go so here are a few notes that might help.

- To start, just choose a site, download it and you're now ready to pick an avatar and a username.
- Until you are ready to deposit, you can play for free at the play money tables and in freerolls.
- You will be able to sort out what's of interest to you from what's on offer in the lobby of poker sites by filtering various options.
- You won't have a dealer there to remind you it's your go (although you really should be paying attention to know this). You will have a timer with a certain amount of time to act in each round. When it's getting low it will make a noise to remind you that if you don't make a decision soon you will miss out on having a choice.
- You can pre-select your decision before it's your turn by ticking your choice from options given on your screen e.g. check/fold. It's not always a great idea to use this, though as

it can be clear to others when you're pre-selecting by how fast the action is made when it comes around to you. If they get a read on when you do this as opposed to when you don't, you could be giving valuable information away.

- There is usually a chat function where you can talk to others at the table and observers. You can also normally block them if they are annoying you.
- You can make online notes about the players around you. The next time you meet them, the note will be there to help remind you of the kind of player they are or an experience you had with them.
- Whatever you win in a tournament will go into your online account (not your bank account) automatically. If you decide to leave a cash game table, then what you have when you left goes back into your poker account.
- You can usually look up past hands to better analyse your play.
- You can look up opponents or friends if you know their player ID.
- You can play formats of poker that would be near impossible to play live e.g. PokerStars' Zoom or Rush at Full Tilt Poker. Rush speeds you to another table as soon as you fold or are finished with a hand, making sure you are always in the action.
- Many sites offer promotions or schemes which reward you for your playing time or for completing certain achievements.

Why play online?

Katie Stone, founder of The Grindettes, is a talented poker player and chess entrepreneur. Here is what she had to say about playing online...

'When I first started playing poker, I played almost strictly live games and thought little of the online poker wizards who existed in a completely different world. The notion of playing poker without seeing someone's face in front of me seemed trivial and suspect. However, friends I had grown up playing chess with (who had also begun playing poker), convinced me of how valuable online poker was not only as an earning mechanism but as the ultimate learning tool as well.

I began playing online poker full-time in January 2010. I found that online poker was different from live poker in many ways, which proved to be very difficult at times, but I also understood quickly how lacking my fundamentals were. For the first five months or so, I struggled and was mainly break-even. About half-way through the year, things started to click for me and the rest of the year went pretty well!

I would not be a professional poker player today, had I not begun to play online poker. There are many reasons why online poker is so great, but here are my top ones as they relate specifically to being a woman:

1. Beginners can learn how to play poker in the comfort of their own home and without fear of judgment or awkward situations with strangers at the live poker table. This is especially valuable for women who may not want to spend their time around a mostly male population in the poker room. Another benefit for beginners playing online is that you can be assured that the rules of the game you are playing will always be followed and the dealer will never

make a mistake! This is helpful in learning the mechanics of cash games and tournaments.

2. Playing online allows you to play the many different variants of poker that you may not find in the live setting. It's not always possible to find a $2/$4 limit hold 'em game in a casino, but you'll always be able to find one online! Every form of poker is offered online making it the ideal way to learn all the different forms.

3. Practice makes perfect, and there is no difference when it comes to poker. When we play online poker we are seeing so many more hands in any given period of time than we would in a live poker setting. The more hands we see, the more times we go deep in a tournament, and the more experience we get playing a short stack, the better our overall game gets.

4. Beginners can benefit from being able to start out playing lower stakes online than in a casino. Most poker rooms don't offer games lower than $1/$2. This can be difficult for a beginner who is concerned about their bankroll. Games as small as $.01/$.02 can be found at any time online giving players the satisfaction of playing for real money without the stress of losing too much while they learn the game.

5. There are many tools used for online poker improvement that helps our overall game. Being able to look back at a complete hand history of a tournament you just played is one of the most valuable tools online poker offers. In addition, different types of software help you understand things like equity and hand ranges, as well as keep notes on your opponents and their tendencies.

6. The Pyjama Factor. This one is huge. I love being able to play poker in my pyjamas and not have to worry what my hair looks like! I also enjoy not having to drive all the way to a casino to play. The comfort factor and ease of access is so attractive for women beginners in particular because of how convenient and worry-free it is.'

Tips for playing online

For a beginner, online poker offers a good environment for trial, error and experimentation.

Age, race, gender or social status has no bearing on whether a person can play poker or not, but people, as they will, tend to judge each other and put one another into boxes regardless. Online poker removes all of this with the presence of the computer screen. The anonymity of playing online can mean amateurs feel more confident in making more aggressive moves or trying out new formats and games. Don't forget, however, that if you've bought in for real money then that's exactly what you're playing with – despite not committing the physical act of putting your hand in your pocket and handing over the cash. You may not be physically holding the chips, but they represent something real, just as they do in live games.

With research showing just how popular online gaming is with women, it's clear that the convenience and nature of online poker is a major draw. Danielle Andersen is a female pro, who for a long time made a living from playing online. When the legal situation in the U.S. made it impossible for her to continue to play online she hit the live scene with fervour. She was featured in a movie called *Bet, Raise, Fold* and now represents online poker site, Ultimate Poker. Here are her crucial tips for playing online:

- Avoid 'tilt' (the physical and mental state that negatively impacts decision-making). Let's be real, losing isn't fun. It's even less fun when losing means your wallet is lighter. When the cards (or opponents) just aren't cooperating, it's easy to become frustrated. When frustrated, it's easier to make that hero call you know can't ever be right. When you make that frustration hero call, you get even more annoyed and you make that bluff against the guy that's never ever folding. You start becoming desperate, and soon you can't even see straight because the steam coming out of your ears is fogging up your vision. Frustration can lead to huge leaks in your game.

- Play fewer tables and pay attention to your opponents. As you get more comfortable you can add tables, but to start, pay attention to what your opponents are doing. How did they size their bet when they had a very strong hand? How about when they missed their draws? If they bet on the flop, do they always continue on the turn and river? How about when they missed their draw and bluffed? People often think when playing online poker, it's impossible to pick up a tell. That's not true. Players will often have consistent tendencies with bet sizing and the timing of their bets that can make the difference between a profitable call or fold.

I have a monster hand. Your hand is even bigger. We're all-in now, our cards are on their backs, and it all boils down to this one moment in time. There's a big inhalation of air as the river is turned over and… BOOM! The underdog comes to the fore and scoops the colossal-sized pot.

That's often the picture of poker painted in the movies. Sensational to the untrained eye, but sadly unrealistic to anyone who plays poker. However, it has to be a good thing if poker gets a look-in and you just can't help but get caught up in some of the old greats and classic clichés.

The 60s gave us movies like *The Cincinnati Kid* and *Cool Hand Luke*. Prisoner Luke Jackson played by Paul Newman stirs up trouble in a game of Five-Card Stud. There's only really a glimpse of poker in this classic but it's a great scene and even features a 'One Time'. This is something you will hear poker players say often when they are looking for play to go their way. In real life, there would be uproar if onlookers were included in the decisions made at the poker table but Luke's prison-mates get away with it here.

'Sometimes nothin' can be a real cool hand', Jackson famously utters, earning him the respect of his fellow inmates and, of course, his eponymous nickname.

The Cincinnati Kid is a classic movie that revolves around poker. The Kid, played by blue-eyed wonder Steve McQueen will, as the movie cover says, 'take on anyone at anything, anytime' in his journey to beat the best in the game. McQueen's character pursues his dream of winning honestly and fairly, with many an adventure and distraction along the way.

While we're in this era, then you have to check out *The Sting* – a classic featuring Robert Redford, Paul Newman and Robert Shaw. Poker isn't a pivotal part but it does feature. It's a good movie about conmen and redemption that will do nicely on a Sunday afternoon.

Moving forward in time, we bump into movies like *Maverick* and *Rounders*. *Maverick*, one of my personal favourites, is another story about a card player trying to prove he is the best there is. Here we see yet another blue-eyed boy as the lead role. Bret Maverick, played by Mel Gibson, meets Annabelle Bransford (Jodie Foster) and we follow their quest to accumulate the funds to enter the All Rivers Draw Poker Championship. Although poker is still trapped in the confines of crime, cheating, and shady behaviour, and the representations of the game and its components are at times farcical, this movie is a whole lot of fun.

Now for 1998 and a great little movie called *Rounders*. It may have not done wonderfully at the time but it's considered a cult classic. Representing just how exhilarating and intense poker can be, the movie revolves around the underground world of poker and is based on Matt Damon and Edward Norton's attempts to pay off a debt using their skills. The villain in the movie is Teddy 'KGB', a Russian mobster who runs an underground game. Often thought of as the best poker movie ever made, it inspired many names we know in the game today to begin their poker journey. There have been rumours about a sequel but we'll just have to wait and see.

chapter 7

Playing in Tournaments

Tournament types and features

There are many different types of poker tournaments available both online and live. Which one you choose to play may depend on the amount of time you have to spare, the kind of event you're in the mood for, or perhaps there's a format you simply feel you have an edge in.

A poker tournament can include any number of players from just two (heads-up) to thousands. They can be single table (STT) or multi-table (MTT). STTs never have more than 10 players sitting at a table and you will rarely see more than nine. There may be a cap on the amount of entrants that can register for a particular event or it could be open to as many as can fit in the room. Day 1 could even be chopped up into one, two, three, even four starting days if needs be (Day 1a, 1b, 1c, 1d etc.). The survivors will then combine for day 2 when all day 1s are complete.

'Flighted' tournaments are another way to include as many players as possible in multi-table tournaments and you can find these on some of the most popular online poker sites. A flighted tournament could have any number of flights (flight 1a, 1b, 1c and so on). These flights may take place on different days at different times to ensure players from all over the world have the chance to join in at a time that is more convenient for them.

Tournaments can sometimes have a guarantee attached to them. This could be any amount that a site or sponsor is willing to promise. This amount is what players will be playing for a share in regardless of how many show up and buy in or qualify; if a guarantee is not reached because fewer players show up than are required to hit the necessary amount, there will be an 'overlay'. This means that additional money will be paid out, at the sponsor's expense.

A popular tournament format is the 'freezeout'. This means what you spend buying-in to the tournament is all you will spend. There are no top-ups, add-ons, or rebuys and when you're out, you're out. Rebuy events give players the ability to buy in again when they are either low on, or just out of, chips. The rebuy period normally lasts for a specific amount of time early on in the tournament; once this time has passed, if you're out of chips, you're out of the tournament. Rebuys can be unlimited during this time or there may be a set amount.

Re-entry events allow you to enter the event again either after you bust or on another starting day. Multi-entry events give players the opportunity to buy into the same event more than once at the same time – this obviously only occurs online where you can play more than one table at a time. On that note, I have seen many professionals play multi-tables live – but when they do this they are playing in different events and running across the room to their seats to their spot in each. Madness!

'Deepstack' tournaments give players a good bit of play i.e.

room for plenty of hands, plenty of betting and the chance to escape a risky situation or mistake or two without losing all your chips. The starting stack is usually quite hefty in comparison to the blinds, and the blinds start small with levels of a nice lengthy duration. If you're looking for a deepstack tournament, you should be prepared for a long ride.

'Turbo' tournaments offer quick, intense action whereby players must accumulate chips as fast as possible in order to progress. Levels are shorter than standard tournaments, so the blinds increase at a faster rate. If you feel the need for

additional speed there are also hyper turbos.

Sit and Gos are another popular tournament format. This kind of tournament kicks off as soon as a specific amount of seats are filled e.g. if it's a nine-handed (nine-person table) Sit and Go then the first hand will be dealt shortly after the ninth player takes his or her seat. Sit and Gos can comprise just one table or multiple tables.

There are also 'shootout' events where each table plays like a separate tournament. There can only be one winner from each table and these winners then go up against each other until just one player is left standing.

Finally, tournaments can feature 'bounties' or 'scalps'. In events that feature bounties, there will be a certain amount of players taking part who have a prize or cash on their heads. If you knock one out, you get to keep the bounty. With scalp tournaments, there may be a prize for the person who knocks out the most players i.e. takes the most scalps, or you may receive money or a prize for every scalp you take in the tournament.

This kind of feature is like seasoning – a little extra spice and competition to keep things interesting. Speaking of which, there are also 'last-longer' bets which see players bet against each other as to who is going to outlast who in a particular event. Sites have taken this concept and made it even bigger by creating a tournament within a tournament and offering a big prize to the last online qualifier (from that specific site) who is left standing in a particular live event.

As you can see there are a whole load of tournaments to choose from and each format and feature means you will have to adjust your strategy. It also means you will never run out of options and will always have something new to try.

Playing in Tournaments

Cash games

I was always a cash game girl. I would come in, play for the length of time I felt comfortable with, and leave with my money whenever I wanted.

I usually decided I was going to play with a certain amount of money and if I lost it, I would go home. Sometimes I would have to sit down at cash game tables with a little more money than planned due to the size of the stacks around me – this is something you should look at when joining a game. Most of the time if I sat down and was much shorter-stacked than others at the table, I would be pushed around by the big guns simply by the force of their ammunition and not so much by the skill behind it. This was not always so bad; I just played quite tight to begin with and then as I built my stack I would loosen up. I sometimes liked to challenge myself to build up a certain amount from the minimum required to buy in. Remember if you find yourself with a shorter than average stack at a cash table or in a tournament, all is not lost. You can apply pressure and do some good damage. Your opponents should worry that at any time you will be ready to make a move. Anyone can be a short-stack ninja!

Obviously, having a lot of chips is preferable, but sometimes people do not know how to adjust when they build a stack. So many times I have seen players splurge their new stack because they feel like they should be making more moves, keeping up the pressure, calling the short stacks and taking chances. You won't have those chips for long if you think that you no longer have to pick your spots.

Tournament winners can take home hefty scores, more than a good night on the cash tables... that is unless you're playing the ridiculous high-stakes cash games in Macau that are rumoured to see millions exchange hands every game! While tournaments can be played in both a single-table format and multi-table format, cash games are played on just one table. In cash games, the chips in front of you are a direct representation of the same amount in good old-fashioned cold, hard cash. That differs from a tournament where everyone gets the same starting stack (there are some exceptions to this e.g. early-to-register bonuses), and the chips do not equal a certain amount in cash. In tournaments you purchase your seat and you will play until you have all the chips or none of them.

Another difference between cash games and tournaments concerns the blinds. In a cash game, the blinds stay the same throughout, whereas in tournaments they increase incrementally as the tournament progresses. You choose your cash game table based on what stakes you feel most

comfortable playing, and that doesn't change unless you change games. When you lose or drop below a certain amount, you can buy in again or top up. When you win, be gracious and don't just skedaddle. Stick around for a little while giving your opponents the chance to win their money back and then politely make your excuses and enjoy your winnings.

Cash games can be found online and live at a wide range of stakes and formats. Playing cash games and playing tournaments require very different approaches to strategy and not all players are good at both. Although tactics differ, there are very many skills that should be developed and applied across all types and formats of games, both online and live. For example, you need to have the same level of focus, concentration, patience, and observation no matter what you play.

Just do me a favour and have a plan when you hit the cash game tables. The last thing you want to become at a poker table is the local ATM!

Ladies-only tournaments

In the past, I have debated the existence of ladies-only events and whether or not they aid or hurt our journey towards equality and recognition.

The very fact that these events separate the sexes and are not an open-playing field, as poker should be, gets to me, but at the same time I have played, and probably will continue to play, in these tournaments. On the other side of the argument lies the fact that women often feel more comfortable playing among other women, especially in the early stages, and it can be a great place to gain confidence in one's live play. I have heard throughout my time in poker that ladies-only events have been very useful in bringing new players into the game, so if the existence of these gender-based events means more female players enter the live poker realm, then they should not be written off. I would say, however, that men shouldn't be playing such events thinking they are going to get value by simply being the only, or one of the only, male players in the room. I have even seen men dress as women while playing ladies-only events... it's not pretty. I don't care how good your legs are guys, leave the women to it and stick with the open events!

Another thing that gets under my skin is the celebration of the last woman standing in a major open-field event. Everyone claps as the last woman hits the rail. Ugh... it makes me shudder. Although, if it means that the extra media coverage this lady gets has a snowball effect and inspires other women to give poker a go, then I guess that's useful for now.

I have been invited to play various ladies-only events and have always had a blast. I've done well in some of these events and found that of the final tables I've experienced, there was a good mix of excellent players and some fast learners who were eager for more experience. Everywhere I've played these events, from Europe to the US, I have had

Playing in Tournaments

the same general experience – the field is not worse or better than the kind of open tournaments that also attract beginners. In my opinion, ladies' events attract a hefty number of beginners and so the field in the earlier stages of these tournaments can be softer than some other live events. This does not represent how females play in general. Yes, I have come across amateur players and some very random players, but the same could be said of various open events I've played in the past.

Ladies' events may be a nice way to start playing live, and can also be a fun, social thing to do, but what will really help you improve your game is to get out there and play in open events. It may seem intimidating at first but you'll soon realise that the weapons your opponents have at their disposal are the same as what you have, except maybe you have the added bonus of using the female stereotype grenade against those who have certain expectations or ideas about how you will play.

The poker world witnesses incredible achievements all the time. Whether it's title-collecting like the select group who have won the triple crown (this means winning a WPT, a WSOP and an EPT title) or the first player in history to win two EPT titles – the incredible Vicky Coren – or how about Phil Hellmuth who has 13 WSOP bracelets to his name?! Poker sees amazing, record-breaking feats all the time, like when Phil 'The Unabomber' Laak set a new Guinness World Record when he played poker for 115 hours straight, or when French pro Bertrand 'ElkY' Grospellier registered for 62 turbo Sit and Gos online, playing as many as 30 at the same time, and finishing in profit within an hour.

Then there are wonderful people like Brother Kevin Crowley, whose Capuchin Centre feeds the homeless in Dublin, Ireland. He often delves into the poker world by working with various sponsors to create Poker For The Homeless tournaments. There are also organisations that get involved, such as Poker Gives and Ante Up For Africa, a Non-Profit Organisation founded by Don Cheadle, Annie Duke and Norman Epstein, which is dedicated to raising money and awareness for those in need in Africa.

The poker community is powerful. This was recently seen in the wake of Typhoon Haiyan when players and staff from Rational Group's Full Tilt Poker and PokerStars raised $280,039.13, which was matched by the Rational Group.

Antonio 'The Magician' Esfandiari tops the all-time money list in poker with live earnings of more than $26 million. Well-known for his slick, laid-back manner, table talk and former magic career, Antonio has amassed many titles. He really hit the jackpot in 2012, when he won over $18 million for taking down the Big One for One Drop at the WSOP. The buy-in was the highest in history at $1 million, with $111,111 of it going to One Drop, a non-profit organization dedicated to worldwide access to clean water. This resulted in One Drop receiving the largest single donation in its history - more than $6 million.

Who could forget the year Jamie Gold won the WSOP Main Event? It was Gold's style of relentlessly forcing his opponents to make a decision, plus his table-talk tactics and controversial plays that got him huge attention. His $12 million first-place prize in 2006 was the

Playing in Tournaments

biggest in WSOP Main Event history.

The biggest pot ever won on TV poker came in 2009 at the Full Tilt Poker Million Dollar Cash Game. Tom Dwan got the better of Phil Ivey taking a pot worth $1.1 million with 7h 6h versus Ivey's Ac 2d after explosive action on a Jc 5c 3d 4h Jh board. The all-in move came from Ivey on the turn as he had a straight to the 5. However, Dwan's seven-high straight was good for the win. A sensational moment in poker – go check it out on YouTube!

The biggest online pot was won by tennis-turned-poker star Patrik Antonius. The Finn beat Swedish online phenomenon Viktor 'Isildur1' Blom in an online hand in 2009, taking down a pot worth over $1.3 million.

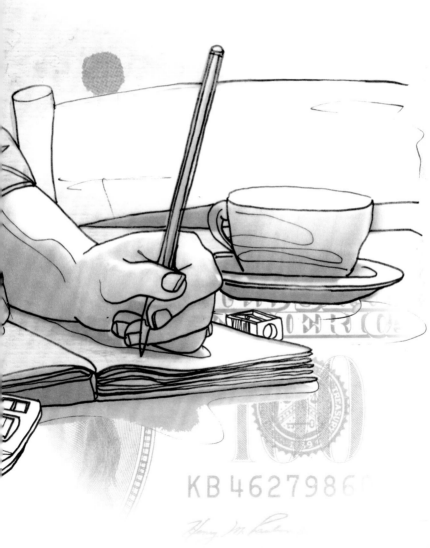

chapter 8

Survival Tips

Staying calm

The poker table is not a scary place to be. In fact, it's a lot of fun and you can take whatever you want out of your time at it. I often get really excited and a little anxious in the moments leading up to play. It takes me a few hands before I find my 'centre' and am at ease. What I've worked on is my frame of mind; I definitely can't perform to the best I can if I'm all worked up.

The day ahead, the play ahead, the moment ahead could be the best one ever. So why not go into it as if that's exactly what it is? This is something poker player and journalist Kara Scott has worked on over time. Growing up, Kara stressed about exams and deadlines and was always looking to do better. This made her extremely driven, but she realises now she was mostly running on terror. Over the years she learned how to get out of her own way and see things from a different perspective.

She says, 'For me, getting over my nerves came down to one really excellent piece of advice that I received years ago. When I was at the beginning of my TV career, a mentor of mine told me that fear and excitement cause very similar responses in your body. Adrenaline and the physical "fight or flight" response will show up whether you're terrified or exhilarated – it doesn't differentiate between the two. What makes the difference between people who are thrill seekers versus those who are thrill avoiders, is simply a matter of perspective. If I could just try to see my own "fear response" as excitement instead of terror, then maybe I wouldn't get so wound up with nerves that I wasn't able to do my job. If I viewed my accelerated heart beat and sweaty palms as indicators of healthy anticipation rather than a clear-cut sign that I would forget all of my lines once the cameras were turned on, then maybe I could actually start to welcome that fluttering feeling that I'd always dreaded.'

Kara mentions one specific fear that can make everything more difficult – fear of failure. Getting over this fear helped Kara in every aspect of her life, including poker. She says, 'If you're nervous to put money into a pot or to lose a hand, then you'll miss out on some great opportunities to win. Believe me, losing happens all the time whether you're just starting out or whether you're a multiple bracelet winner! Taking the fear away from a "big risk" in poker meant that I could look at situations more logically and methodically. Keeping composure at the poker table is a key skill. If fear and discomfort are written all over your face, then you're handing your opponents the tools to beat you. They'll be able to push you off hands when scary flops come down and they'll also have a good idea of when you're holding a strong hand, as they'll be watching out for those tell-tale signs of anxiety. You never want to give your opponents that kind of information.'

Nowadays, playing in a major tournament can sometimes mean opening yourself up to a wider audience. With the presence of TV, live streaming, live blogging and online videos, how you decide to play a hand in one moment can stick with you for years to come. Kara says, "I've played some absolute stinkers but accepting that you'll make mistakes is an important part of the process of getting better. Being scared to make the wrong moves could lead to being scared to make any moves at all! The way I see it, if my opponents know about hands that I misplayed years ago, they might just underestimate me and that is always welcome.'

Top tips

Aside from the more technical aspects of poker, there are many things you can do on and off the felt to be a better player or to at least give you a better chance of being successful. A lot of them concern our mental and physical approach, which often affects the outcome of anything we do in life.

The Wrath of Boredom

Although poker is a fun and exciting game, there are many dull moments where you are not involved in the action or you're feeling tired or bored. It's hard to concentrate all the time but disconnecting from the zone can easily lead to distraction or mistakes. For example, you start chatting or playing with your phone. While this is happening, you can miss out on information or opportunity. It works both ways though – plenty of players get bored and give information away. If you find you have not been active for a while, another thing that might happen is that you start getting involved out of boredom or out of fear you're becoming predictable. If you're calling with something you would not be happy to see a raise with, and you have no plan as to what you're going to do next, then just fold. Be patient and pick your spots, you don't have to get involved all the time.

Learning Lessons

Most professionals will say that they are still learning each and every day they play. In poker as in life, the best lessons I have learned are through the mistakes I've made. In fact I wish there was a better word for them. 'Mistake' carries the negative connotation of something that shouldn't have happened or something you would erase if you could. But how would you know to do it differently or better in the future if it didn't exist? If you can learn to see mistakes as lessons then you won't be so hard on yourself. It's never fun getting knocked out of a tournament but if I feel I played well then it makes it a little easier. I allow myself to agonise about it for a little while but there's a point when it's time to let it go. What really gets to me is if I believe I didn't play to the best of my abilities. I feel I let myself down and blew the opportunity. The only way to make something good out of this is to look at what you believe you could have done better and do it next time.

No Shame in Folding

If you make a move and someone plays back at you and you are uncomfortable with the situation, then why not wait until you are more comfortable to get involved. Folding doesn't mean that you're weak or that someone has outplayed you or is better than you. Don't let pride or ego get in the way of your decision-making process. If you watch professionals play, you will rarely see them take a long time to fold or agonise about mucking their cards – unless it's in a really close scenario with a lot on the line or they feel they have committed themselves in a tricky spot. What you will see often is a professional instantly folding, even though they may have been the original aggressor in the situation. It's just another part of poker. Folding doesn't mean you're handing away control. In fact you're maintaining it. After all, it was part of your overall plan, wasn't it?

Planning Ahead

That brings me to the next topic – planning. Try to have a plan for what you're going to do based on your stack size, your position and those of your opponents. You can also have plans when it comes to hands you get involved in. This will give you more confidence at the felt and a greater sense of satisfaction with the decisions you make. If you have a plan and are willing to react to what others do instead of just sticking brazenly to your intentions, then you can make the most of your decisions – this may also mean folding later in the hand to escape loss. Your plan should not be too strict. Instead of 'I'm going to do X, Y and then Z' it should be 'I'll do X and if Y happens I'll do Z; if it doesn't I'll do Y.' Always good to have a back-up plan, right?

Setting Goals

Having a goal in poker is really helpful when it comes to maintaining focus. It is also useful in quantifying your own personal successes. How you choose your goals is up to you but I would advise making them less to do with how much money you made or where you finished and more to do with personal achievements like honing a particular skill or strengthening a weakness. In the poker world you will often hear stories of how player A has bet player B that he can't lose a certain amount of weight in a certain amount of time or that he can't win a certain amount of WSOP bracelets or he can't go a year without alcohol, for example. If it's about improving your health, then I say go ahead, but if the incentive is purely monetary, the results may not be long-lived. Goals should come from within and lead to something that only you can truly benefit from.

Chess champion, poker player, author and all-round bright spark Jennifer Shahade, says, 'Set goals that are not based on money but play i.e. how hard you can focus, paying attention to showdowns, focusing on bet sizing, or finding good spots to bluff. Try to pick a goal like that rather than "I want to win X amount of buy-ins this session", because in live play the sample sizes are so small you really can't control results. Why not attempt something simple like trying to have a good time without giving information away. That way you can be happy with yourself and your play even if you don't win. Sometimes I have great days in terms of winning, but I still don't let myself feel fully happy because I didn't meet playing-quality goals. Other times I feel amazing after busting because I played well. It's a fight against being results-oriented; it's very tough to avoid thinking that if you're on a hot streak or cold streak you're playing great or badly respectively, especially because of external forces. If you want to get better at poker you have to really consciously fight this mentality, in my opinion. Although obviously you should win money ultimately if you're playing well!'

Your Wealth and Your Health

I have always kept my poker money separate from the rest of my incomings and outgoings and I would recommend any player to do the same. Obviously full-time professionals may have a different way of doing this but as a beginner you should decide what you're comfortable spending and then go from there. What's in my poker bankroll does not determine how well I'm playing, like Jennifer says above, but it can determine what events I play and levels I play at. Paying close attention to your wins and losses is key in understanding the kinds of games you should be playing. If you're not winning at the current level you're playing at then it's not really the time to move up. I've seen players do this to recoup their losses, but this doesn't always work out and can lead to a terrible downward spiral. We all take risks but if we want to have fun playing poker, while also using it to add some extra padding to our bank accounts, then we have to respect our bankroll and pay close attention to what's going out as well as what's going in.

Now, go get 'em!

A lot can be learned about life at the poker table, and a lot can be learned about poker in life. More and more I realise that like so many people and personalities seated around one table, put together by chance, with various game plans and goals in mind, life can often be compared to a big ol' game of cards. It's about avoiding distraction and staying focused on what is straight ahead of you; it's about choosing your battles and not letting egos (your own or others') get in the way of your goal; it's learning from your mistakes but also allowing yourself to move on from them; it's celebrating your successes and remembering them as much as, if not more than, your failures; it's finding out strengths and weaknesses – most importantly your own.

Everyone is different, so in order to be able to work/live/play together, we have to try and figure out the best way to approach and interact with each other. The same approach does not work with everyone so perception is often very important; taking the time to gather as much information as possible in order to navigate our way to where we want to go. There is so much information out there for the taking. However, sometimes you just have to fake it to make it, and that's when it's time to work on your poker face.

Being part of the poker world is something I wouldn't ever change. The characters, the places, the stories… it is a very ordinary community living a very extraordinary existence.

The game brings people of all races, ages, and backgrounds together. Often like a traveling circus, the same faces set up shop all around the world in search of the next champion. Now with online poker, more and more people have the opportunity to see places they had never been and have experiences they will not quickly forget.

I started playing poker just before the boom when it was rare to see a woman, never mind a young woman, spend her Friday nights slumming it with the boys at the cash tables. A lot has changed since then, even with the game itself, but a few things have stayed true – the relentless passion for the sense of competition, the love of testing one's mettle against another, the enjoyment of spending time learning lessons and stories about ourselves and others, the search for self-improvement and the hope for those times when skill and a pinch of luck result in a well-deserved win...

Ah – the sound of the chips clattering against each other, the crisp shirt of the dealer as he or she cuts a freshly opened deck, the introductions, the judgments, the transition from strangers to friends ... and also enemies, the anticipation of what is going to happen next, and the hunt to be the best based purely on your own merits. Welcome, new friend, take your seat and let's get this game underway. It's time to shuffle up and deal.

Survival Tips

Index

Ace-high 53
aggressive players 25
all-in 37, 46, 47, 87, 102
Andersen, Danielle 100
Ante Up for Africa 114
antes 84
Antonius, Patrik 115
Aussie Millions 83

Bet, Raise, Fold (film) 100
betting 44–45, 46–47, 60, 85, 91, 101, 109
big blind 41, 44, 45, 46, 81
'big slick' 59
biggest wins 114–115
Binion, Benny 20
blinds 41, 42, 44–45, 46, 59, 80, 81, 84, 107, 111
Blom, Viktor Isildur1 115
bluffing 66–67, 69, 100, 101
Boeree, Liv 23, 29
bounty tournaments 109
Brunson, Doyle ("Texas Dolly") 38
bubble, the 81
buck, the 36
burning 37
button (dealer button) 41, 42, 89

Calling 44, 45, 59, 60, 61, 85, 87, 100, 101
card marking 37

Card Player magazine and website 22
cash games 110–111
celebrity poker pros 16
Chantler, Gareth 60
charity work 114
Cheadle, Don 114
checking 44, 45, 85
Cincinnati Kid (film) 102, 103
community cards 14, 37, 46, 62
Cool Hand Luke (film) 102
Coren, Vicky 22–23, 29, 114
'cowboys' 59
Crowley, Brother Kevin 114
cutoff 42–43, 89

Damon, Matt 58, 103
De Melo, Fatima Moreira 70–71, 82
dealer 84
dealing 36
deepstack tournaments 107
Diamond, Lou 11
draw poker 14
Duke, Annie 21, 114
Dwan, Tom 115

Eolis, Wendeen 20–21
Epstein, Norman 114
equity 62–63
Esfandiari, Antonio The Magician 114

ESPN 33
etiquette 84–85, 87
European Poker Tour (EPT) 22–23, 29, 83, 114

Fifth street 37
five-betting 17, 44
Five-Card Draw 14
Five-Card Stud 14, 102
Fixed Limit Hold 'em 46, 47
flighted tournaments 106
floating 17
flop, the 14, 37, 46, 59, 62, 63, 89, 101, 119
flop poker 14, 15
Flush 51
folding 36, 37, 44, 85, 91, 101, 121
Foster, Jodie 103
four-betting 44
Four-of-a-kind (quads) 50
fourth street 37
Freer, Barbara 20
freerolls 94, 96
freezeout 107
Full House (boat) 50
Full Tilt Poker 114

Gibson, Mel 103
Gold, Jamie 115
Grindettes, The 31, 98
Grospellier, Bertrand Elky 114

Hand, the 36
hand ranking system 48
Harman, Jennifer 21, 28
having position 43

heads up 40, 81, 106
Hellmuth, Phil 114
hijack 42
history of poker 10–11
hole cards 14, 36, 46, 58, 59, 62

In position 43, 89
Ivey, Phil 115

Jenkins, Ben 88–91

Kicker 50

Laak, Phil 114
'ladies', the 59
ladies-only tournaments 112–113
last-longer bets 109
Liebert, Kathy 28
Liu, Xuan 82–83
live poker
  beginners 90–91
  entering the real world 78–79
  a live tournament 80–83
loose aggressive (LAG) players 25
loose passive players 25
loose players 24

McQueen, Steve 103
mathematics of poker 60–61
Maverick (film) 103
mining 59
Moneymaker, Chris 10, 11, 13, 38
movies 102–103
'muck', the 36, 37, 85
multi-entry events 107

125

Index

multi-table tournament (MTT) 106, 107

Naujoks, Sandra 23, 29
Newman, Paul 102, 103
No-Limit Texas Hold 'em (NLH) 46, 88
Norton, Edward 103

Obrestad, Annette 29
Omaha 14
One Pair 53
online poker 10, 16, 17, 22, 90
    the biggest pot 115
    how it works 96–97
    online tips 100–101
    poker rooms 94
    tournaments 94–95, 97
    why play online 98–99
outs 63

Pacific Poker Tour 83
PaddyPowerPoker.com 32
PartyPoker.com 32, 33
    The Big Game 33
    Premier League 33
passing the buck 36
passive players 25
playing styles 24–25
'pocket rockets' 59
poker boom 17, 22
Poker for the Homeless tournaments 114
Poker Gives 114
poker jargon 54–55
Poker Night Live (TV show) 32, 33
poker odds calculator 59
Poker PROductions 33
poker software 17
poker table
    how it is set up 40–41
    positions at the table 42–43
PokerStars online poker site 11, 28, 29, 114
pot, the 37, 43, 46, 47, 81, 85, 88, 89
    biggest 115
    odds 60–61, 62
Pot-limit Hold 'em 46–47
prejudice, overcoming 30–31

Raising 44, 45, 60, 85, 87
Rational Groups 114
re-entry events 107
re-raising 44
rebuy events 107
Redford, Robert 103
Richmond, Vera 20
river, the 14, 37, 46, 60, 62, 88, 89, 101, 102, 115
Rounders (film) 38, 58, 103
Rousso, Vanessa 29
Royal Flush 49

Satellites 94–95
scalp tournaments 109
Scott, Kara 32–33, 118–119
Selbst, Vanessa 21, 28, 29
Seven-Card Stud 14–15
Shahade, Jennifer 122–123
Shaw, Robert 103

shootout events 109
single-table tournament (STT) 106
Sit and Go tournaments 109
Slim, Amarillo 38
slow roll 87
small blinds 41, 44, 45, 46
starting hands 58–59
stealing 42, 43
Sting, The (film) 103
Stone, Katie 31, 70, 98
Straight 49, 51
Straight Flush 49
strategy 58–59
string betting 85
stud poker 14
success stories 28–29
suited broadways 89
suited connectors 59, 89
survival tips
  staying calm 118–119
  top tips 120–123

Team Party 32
tells (reads) 64–65, 91, 101
Texas Hold 'em 14, 15, 31
  betting 44–45
  the hands 48–53
  introducing 38–39
  poker ingredients 36–37
  positions at the table 42–43
  table set-up 40–41
  variants 46–47
Three of a kind 52
three-betting 44
tight aggressive (TAG) players 25
tight passive players 25, 27
tight players 24
tips for beginners 88–91
  keep things simple 88–89
  play the good hands 89
  play your hands in position 89
  playing live 90–91
tournament play
  biggest wins 114–115
  cash games 110–111
  ladies–only 112–113
  types and features 105–106, 109
triple crown 114
turbo tournaments 107, 109
turn, the 14, 37, 46, 101
TV poker 10, 11, 13, 29, 38
  biggest pot 115
Two Pair 52

Ultimate Poker site 100
under the gun (UTG) 42
under the gun +1 42

Weisner, Melanie 43, 71–72
Whitton, Charlotte 21
women players
  arrival of 20–21
  breaking the gender barrier 22–23
  femininity, using your 70–73
  preconceptions about 26–27
World Poker Tour (WPT) 83, 114
World Series of Poker (WSOP) 10–11, 20, 21, 29, 33, 114, 115

Index

Acknowledgments

A big thank you to the wonderfully talented designer Barbara Zuniga, Rachel Parsons for her amazingly artistic illustrations and Leslie Harrington for coordinating the design and finding Rachel! Big thanks goes to Editorial Director Julia Charles, whose infectious passion and warmth made me feel like part of the team as soon as we met, and Commissioning Editor Nathan Joyce who has been a rock throughout the whole process and an absolute pleasure to work with. Kara Scott, you have been amazing. Katie Stone, thank you for your passion and sharing in my excitement. Fatima Moreira de Melo, Xuan Liu, Danielle Andersen, Jennifer Shahade, and Melanie Weisner – what amazing female talent! I am so happy to feature all your input and insights and really enjoyed our discussions in the making of this. Thank you to Christian Zetzsche for his inspiring photo, and to photographers Danny Maxwell and Ailbe Collins for being there for advice. Ben Jenkins and Gareth Chantler – it's always a pleasure. You're true gents. Dermot Blain, thank you for your eyes and encouragement! I would like to thank the Rational Group for allowing me to spend time on this project when I needed it, particularly Eric Hollreiser. To the friends I missed dates with – I'm free now if you'd like? Vivienne, Roberta, Louise, Molly and Ciara – thank you for the cheerleading and for bearing with me. To my beautiful family – what would I do without you? My sisters Judy and Ruth, and brothers Darren and Jim, your love, support and genuine interest in how everything was going made this so exciting. I can't forget my American family, whose wishes spurred me on from across the seas. Thank you! Last but not least my two amigos, my parents Val and Jim. I can't explain what your love and support means to me. My final thank you goes to my best friend and true love, Wesley Willetts. Your belief in me is what kept me going through this whole project. Thanks for putting up with constant poker talk and my stressed head. And thank you for making me go dancing while I put together my first book, an ambition I've had forever, and that you helped me achieve. I love you.